DANIEL

Encouragement for Faith

Multitudes who sleep in the dust of the earth will awake:
some to everlasting life, others to shame and everlasting contempt.
Those who are wise will shine like the brightness of the heavens, and
those who lead many to righteousness, like the stars for ever and ever.

Daniel 12:2–3

By Paul E. Deterding

CONCORDIA PUBLISHING HOUSE · SAINT LOUIS

Edited by Julene Gernant Dumit

Series editors: Thomas J. Doyle and Rodney L. Rathmann

We solicit your comments and suggestions concerning this material. Please write to Product Manager, Adult Bible Studies, Concordia Publishing House, 3558 S. Jefferson Avenue, St. Louis, MO 63118-3968.

The text for "All You Works of the Lord" (lesson 4) is from *Lutheran Book of Worship* copyright © 1978. Used by permission of Concordia Publishing House. All rights reserved.

Unless otherwise stated, Scripture taken from the HOLY BIBLE, NEW INTERNATIONAL VERSION®. NIV®. Copyright © 1973, 1978, 1984 by International Bible Society. Used by permission of Zondervan Publishing House. All rights reserved.

Biblical references marked RSV are from the Revised Standard Version of the Bible, copyrighted 1946, 1952, ©1971, 1973. Used by permission.

3 4 5 6 7 8 9 10 11   15 14 13 12 11 10 09 08 07 06

Contents

Lesson 1

Introduction and Overview

Theme Verse

While I was still in prayer, Gabriel, the man I had seen in the earlier vision, came to me in swift flight about the time of the evening sacrifice. He instructed me and said to me, "Daniel, I have now come to give you insight and understanding." **(Daniel 9:21–22)**

Goal

In this session we aim to develop an appreciation for the type of literature contained in the book of Daniel as a means by which God communicates to us His message of judgment and salvation. What we learn in this lesson will help us to appreciate the message of Daniel as primarily one of encouragement for God's people to remain in their faith.

What's Going On Here?

Along with the book of Revelation, the average Christian surely finds Daniel to be the most difficult portion of Holy Scripture to understand. The problems that we encounter in interpreting these two books stem, in part, from the fact that both are examples of a type of literature known as "apocalyptic" (a-päk-a-LIP-tik). The Greek word *apocalypsis* (a-päk-a-LIP-sis), meaning "revelation," is the name given to the last book of the Bible in the Greek New Testament, and from it we derive the name *apocalyptic*.

Daniel is an early example of apocalyptic, a type of literature that became more widely used among the Jewish people during the last centuries of the Old Testament era. As an apocalyptic book, Daniel has certain features in common with other apocalyptic writings, including the book of Revelation and a host of nonbiblical documents. Therefore, it is important that we know something about apocalyptic literature in general before we attempt to study one of the biblical apocalyptic writings.

Searching the Scriptures
Characteristics of Apocalyptic Literature

Certain kinds of literature, such as Greek tragedy, are distinguished by certain features common to all examples of that type of literature. Among apocalyptic writings, one can also identify certain common characteristics. In general terms it may be said that apocalyptic is distinguished by the following literary features:

1. *Deliverance from affliction.* Apocalyptic writings generally are written during a time of spiritual affliction. The author takes a limited interest in the events of history and instead looks beyond history to a time of deliverance. For this reason apocalyptic literature stresses the *end times* and the final triumph of God's people. Therefore, the *resurrection* of the dead and the final judgment are frequently prominent themes of apocalyptic writing.

2. *Dualism.* Dualism is the name given to the manner in which apocalyptic writing views the world as caught up in a great struggle between God and those in His camp against all the forces of evil. As a result, *angels* often play a major role in apocalyptic literature. The authors of apocalyptic writings look to a final victory to be won by God on behalf of His people.

3. *God's control.* Despite the seemingly hopeless circumstances in which apocalyptic is written, its message is that God is still in control. We will note a number of examples of this throughout the book of Daniel.

4. *Revelation of divine secrets.* Apocalyptic writings give (or at least claim to give) revelations of *divine secrets* and *mysteries* concerning the current and future status of the world. Often such revelations are communicated by *dreams* or *visions*. As a portion of Holy Scripture, the book of Daniel contains revelations that were given by the triune God and are therefore true and reliable.

5. *Symbolism.* Apocalyptic literature makes extensive use of symbolism that often seems bizarre. Apocalyptic symbols frequently include *beasts* and *numbers*. The symbolic numbers of apocalyptic are often used in a *cosmic calendar* of events leading to the end of time. It is particularly the use of symbolism that makes apocalyptic writing so difficult to understand.

Look up the following passages from Daniel, and note which of the above mentioned characteristics of apocalyptic literature are found in each.

1:17   **2:19**   **2:26**

3:6	3:28	4:9
4:10	4:13	5:16
6:16	6:22	7:1
7:3	7:16	7:25
8:1	8:14	8:16
8:17	9:21	9:24
10:7	10:13	12:1
12:2–4	12:7	

The Interpretation of Apocalyptic Literature

Throughout the history of the Christian church, there have been essentially four different methods proposed for interpreting the apocalyptic writings of the Holy Scriptures:

1. Some argue that the apocalyptic writings described historical events that had already occurred at the time of writing. The real author claimed to be some important individual from the past who had predicted these occurrences. Thus the "prophecy" of apocalyptic was actually written after the fact. While this interpretation holds true for much nonbiblical apocalyptic literature, the Christian confesses that biblical apocalyptic literature is truly prophetic and indeed was written prior to the events it describes as happening in the future.

2. Others see apocalyptic literature as dealing only with what is to take place immediately before and after the end of the world. While apocalyptic does stress the end times, an interpretation like this fails to consider the

historical context out of which a particular apocalyptic writing arose and the message that it had also for the people for whom it was originally written.

3. Still others believe that apocalyptic has nothing to do with actual historical events but merely gives general principles of life. This approach also ignores the original historical circumstances out of which apocalyptic writings arose and overlooks that fact that the Scriptures usually teach general principles by way of specific and concrete events in history.

4. The most satisfying approach is to see apocalyptic literature as a broad sketch of the entire history of God's dealings with His people up to and including the end. This interpretation takes into account both the original circumstances and also the fact that biblical apocalyptic literature speaks to all generations of humanity.

Author

What indication about the authorship of the book of Daniel is given in the following passages: **7:1–2, 28; 8:1, 15; 9:2; 10:2; 12:4, 5?** What information on the identity of the author of this book is given to us in **Matthew 24:15?**

Historical Circumstances

The message of Daniel is more readily understood when we are aware of the political history of the times described by this portion of Scripture.

1. Read **Daniel 7:3, 17.** What is symbolized by the beasts of this vision?

2. Compare **Daniel 7:4** with **4:28–34.** What great world empire is represented by the first beast?

3. Compare **Daniel 7:6** with **8:21–22.** What world empire is symbolized by the third beast?

4. Compare **Daniel 7:5** with **8:5–7, 20.** Of what great world empire is the second beast a symbol?

5. What is said of the fourth beast in **Daniel 7:7?**

Outline

The book of Daniel may be outlined easily, for it divides naturally into two parts. **Chapters 1–6** consist of narratives from the life of Daniel. **Chapters 7–12** recount visions of future world events that were given to him.

Language

The book of Daniel is one of a handful of Old Testament books (the others being Genesis, Jeremiah, and especially Ezra) which contain portions written in Aramaic (a language similar to Hebrew that served as the language of international relations during the times described in Daniel). The Aramaic portion of Daniel begins with the words "O king" in **2:4** and continues until the end of **chapter 7.** There is no apparent reason for the bilingual character of Daniel.

The Word for Us

1. In what ways are the times in which we are living similar to those during which Daniel and other apocalyptic writings were composed?

2. Why do the circumstances in which we live make the message of Daniel particularly applicable to our own daily lives? Why is it that Daniel is relevant to all eras of the existence of the people of God?

3. What are some principles that are important for correctly understanding the book of Daniel?

Closing

Read or sing together the first two stanzas of "I Will Sing My Maker's Praises":

I will sing my Maker's praises
And in Him most joyful be,
For in all things I see traces
Of His tender love to me.
Nothing else than love could move Him
With such deep and tender care
Evermore to raise and bear
All who try to serve and love Him.
All things else have but their hour,
God's great love retains its pow'r.

He so cared for and esteemed me
That the Son He loved so well
He gave for me to redeem me
From the quenchless flames of hell.
O Lord, spring of boundless blessing,
How then could my finite mind
Of Your love the limit find
Though my efforts were unceasing?
All things else have but their hour,
God's great love retains its pow'r.

Lesson 2

The Testing
of the Four Young Men

Theme Verse

Daniel resolved not to defile himself with the royal food and wine, and he asked the chief official for permission not to defile himself this way. Now God had caused the official to show favor and sympathy to Daniel. **(Daniel 1:8–9)**

Goal

We seek to be brought to a greater understanding of how we believers are to live as those who are in the world but not of the world. The Christian's relationship to his or her government is an important part of his life here on this earth, and much of what we will learn today will help us to see how our God would have us live.

What's Going On Here?

Daniel, Hananiah (Shadrach), Mishael (Meshach), and Azariah (Abednego) were among a group of promising, handsome, upper-class young men taken from their homeland to Babylon by Nebuchadnezzar to be trained for his service. Thrust into a foreign culture and forced into a course of study steeped in pagan mythology, magic, and sorcery, these young men, strengthened by their God, remained faithful to Him.

Searching the Scriptures
The Historical Setting

Read **Daniel 1:1–2.** The events recorded here took place in 605 B.C. As we will see in the next verse, Nebuchadnezzar also took some of the inhabitants of Judah with him back to Babylon. This was the first of four deportations of Judeans to Babylon. The others occurred in 597 **(2 Kings 24:8–14; Jeremiah 52:28)**, 586 (when Jerusalem and the temple were destroyed **[2 Kings 25:8–11; Jeremiah 52:29]**), and 581 **(Jeremiah 52:30).** (Those who are interested can consult the information under this section in the leaders notes for information on the various dating systems used in the ancient Near East that account for the differing dates used in **2 Kings** and **Jeremiah**.)

1. In the ancient Near East, if one country defeated another, the gods of the victorious country were seen as superior to those of the defeated country. Keeping that in mind and noting what Nebuchadnezzar took from Jerusalem and what he did with it **(Daniel 1:2)**, what would some people have thought about the God of Judah? How does Daniel make it clear that this was not the case?

2. Why did the Lord deliver Judah to Nebuchadnezzar in this and subsequent years? See **Ezekiel 8:14–18; 9:9–10**.

3. When were the temple articles returned to Jerusalem **(Ezra 1:7–8, 11)**?

Introduction of the Main Characters
Read **Daniel 1:3–7.**

1. How may **1:3** be understood as denoting the fulfillment of a prophecy spoken to Hezekiah and recorded in **Isaiah 39:7**?

Note the NIV text note on **Daniel 1:4.** The word the NIV translates as "Babylonians" in the phrase "language and literature of the Babylonians" is literally the word *Chaldeans. Chaldean* may be used as an ethnic term for the race of people living in Babylon (the word is used this way in **Daniel 9:1**). If it is used in this sense in **Daniel 1:4,** then the young Judeans were to be taught the languages (for example, Sumerian) and literature of Babylon. The term may also be used for a class of wise men (it is used that way in **chapter 2** and translated by the NIV as "astrologers" [for example, **2:2**]). If this is the sense intended in **Daniel 1:4,** the young Judeans were trained to become members of this professional class of wise men.

2. How might this relate to the other narratives in Daniel **(2:13; 4:7–8; 5:11–12)**? What other biblical figure had a similar experience in his youth **(Acts 7:22)**?

3. The names of four Judean youths involved in this training are given: Daniel ("my judge is God"), Hananiah ("the LORD is gracious"), Mishael ("who is what God is"), Azariah ("the LORD has helped"). What was the point of giving them Babylonian names **(Daniel 4:8)**? At what other points in Israel's history did something like this take place **(2 Kings 23:34; 24:17)**?

The Fidelity of the Four Young Men

Read **Daniel 1:8–16.**

1. We don't know for sure exactly why Daniel and his three friends objected to the royal food and wine. What possibilities do the following verses suggest: **Exodus 34:13–16** (especially **verse 15**); **1 Corinthians 10:20–21, 27–29; Leviticus 11:1–4; 17:10–11**?

2. What characteristics did Daniel exhibit when faced with this temptation?

3. What enabled Daniel's plan to succeed? Explain how that happened.

The word translated "vegetables" in **verse 12** can also refer to grains and hence also to breads. The point of this narrative is not to advocate vegetarianism but to demonstrate how the Lord cares for those who are faithful to Him and do not forsake Him for other gods, even when there is grave temptation to forsake Him. The message of **Daniel 1** is to encourage God's people, such as those in exile in Babylon, that it is worthwhile to remain faithful to the God of Judah, regardless of the disadvantages that may come one's way. The four young men were better in appearance than the others because of the Lord's intervention on their behalf.

4. How is this narrative an illustration of **Jeremiah 29:4–7?**

The Progress of the Four Young Men

Read **Daniel 1:17–21.**

1. According to **verse 17** how did this foursome fare in their course of instruction? Who was the source of their progress? Did they uncritically accept all that they were taught by the Chaldeans (see for example, **3:12; 6:12–13**)? What, therefore, was included in the "wisdom" spoken of in this section **(Proverbs 9:10)?**

2. What special gifts distinguished Daniel from the others? How did he use these gifts (**2:17–19, 24; 4:8–9; 5:11–12**)? What gift would this indicate Daniel possessed (**Numbers 12:6; Matthew 24:15**)? What other Old Testament figure in similar circumstances possessed similar gifts (**Genesis 41:15–16**)?

3. To what event does **verse 18** refer (**1:5**)? How did the four young men fare in comparison to the others (**verse 19**)?

4. How did the Lord further bless this foursome (**verse 20**)? How was this eventually recognized (**2:24, 48–49; 3:30**)?

5. Who is the Cyrus spoken of in **verse 21** (**Ezra 1:1**)? Why is the beginning of his reign mentioned here even though Daniel was still alive and apparently active as late as the third year (**10:1**) of his reign? See **Isaiah 44:24–45:3**.

The Word for Us

1. How is this chapter an illustration of what is said in **2 Timothy 2:8–13**? What implications does this have for our life of faith?

2. What guidance do we receive from this chapter of Daniel for those occasions when those over us, such as an employer or even our government, ask us to do something that is contrary to God's will?

3. Many things are neither commanded nor forbidden by God's Word. For example, we are neither commanded nor forbidden to abstain from certain foods **(Romans 14:14).** In such matters believers are free to do as they choose. However, circumstances may affect how they will decide. In the case of the incident in our text, Daniel and his friends abstained from certain foods in part because the eating of them probably involved approval of Babylonian idolatry. How might Christians today find themselves in similar circumstances?

Closing

Sing or read together "Fight the Good Fight":

Fight the good fight with all your might;
Christ is your strength, and Christ your right.
Lay hold on life, and it shall be
Your joy and crown eternally.

Run the straight race through God's good grace;
Lift up your eyes, and seek His face.
Life with its way before us lies;
Christ is the path, and Christ the prize.

Cast care aside, lean on your guide;
His boundless mercy will provide.
Trust, and enduring faith shall prove
Christ is your life and Christ your love.

Faint not nor fear, His arms are near;
He changes not who holds you dear;
Only believe, and you will see
That Christ is all eternally.

Lesson 3

The Fall of World Empires

Theme Verse

"In the time of those kings, the God of heaven will set up a kingdom that will never be destroyed, nor will it be left to another people. It will crush all those kingdoms and bring them to an end, but it will itself endure forever." **(Daniel 2:44)**

Goal

In this lesson we will see how all the might of this world is subject to the God who has revealed Himself to us in the person and work of Jesus Christ.

What's Going On Here?

The time was the second year of Nebuchadnezzar's reign. The relatively new king was in control of a substantial portion of the ancient Near East. But surely he thought about whether he could retain that control. And in a culture that valued dreams highly as a means of foretelling the future, the king had a puzzling dream, of which he demanded to know the meaning.

While this dream turned out to predict no harm to Nebuchadnezzar himself, it did say much about the longevity of his dynasty and the longevity of all kingdoms of the world. In comparison to puny Judah, the might of Babylon seemed supreme. But the God of Judah would have the last word. He Himself would set up a kingdom that would destroy all earthly kingdoms, would fill the earth, and would last forever.

Searching the Scriptures

Nebuchadnezzar's Dream

Read **Daniel 2:1–6.**

This incident took place in Nebuchadnezzar's second year. Whether or not Daniel and his three friends had finished their training (which in **1:5** is described as lasting three years) is an interesting but open question. In the first part of the account Daniel and his friends are not present when the king first speaks with his wise men, but in **2:13** they are numbered among all the wise men of Babylon who are to be killed. The edict could have been so broad as to include wise men in training. Or it could have been that Daniel and his three friends had just finished their training but were not really established.

If this is the case, it is helpful to remember that the Hebrews often counted partial units of time as full ones. So the course of instruction may not have been a full three years but may have spanned three years. (For a parallel see Jesus' statement in **Matthew 12:40.**)

The method of reckoning the year of Nebuchadnezzar's reign may also play into interpretation. Daniel may here be using the "accession year" method (see the leaders notes of lesson 1 under "The Historical Setting," where this is called "method B"). If so, the first year of the training session may have occupied the initial, partial year of Nebuchadnezzar's reign. The first full year of his rule would then be counted as year 1 (corresponding to the second year of the training) and the second full year (corresponding to the final year of the training) as year 2. In any case, it seems that Daniel and his friends were newcomers to the Babylonian court and the workings of its wise men.

It is also interesting in conjunction with the dream to remember that Babylon was at this time displaying considerable military superiority over Judah. The dream of Nebuchadnezzar serves to make the point that the might of the armies and nations of the world will eventually succumb to the might of the Lord.

What was the king's unusual request and to whom did he make it? What threat and promise did he make regarding the answering of his request (**2:5–6;** see also **2 Kings 10:27**)?

The Dilemma of the Wise Men

Read **Daniel 2:7–16.**

1. Compare the language used by the wise men in **verses 7** and **10** with that of **verse 4.** What does this suggest about their attitude before the king? What were they hoping to accomplish by their carefully complimentary words **(2:8)?**

2. What was Nebuchadnezzar's reaction to all of this **(2:12–13)?** Who, therefore, was included in the king's decree?

3. How does Daniel's response to this situation **(2:14–16)** harmonize with the account in the first chapter?

The Revelation

Read **Daniel 2:17–23.**

1. What name is used for Daniel's God in **2:18–19?** What is the significance of using this particular name in this chapter?

2. Whose aid did Daniel seek in his endeavor **(2:17–18)?** How does this serve as an illustration of what is said in **Hebrews 10:25** and **Colossians 4:2–3?**

3. What terms are used in **2:18–19** for the dream and its interpretation? In what way does Paul use these same terms **(Romans 16:25–26; Ephesians 3:3–6)?**

4. What was Daniel's first response when God answered his prayer? Why is it appropriate that mention should be made of "wisdom" and "kings" in **2:20–23?** What evidence is there that Daniel's three friends were still involved with him **(2:23)?**

Daniel's Humility before the King

Read **Daniel 2:24–30.**

1. What rather remarkable fact about the one who would interpret the dream was indicated by Arioch's announcement to the king **(2:25)?** How might this relate to the overall theme of the chapter?

2. How did Daniel demonstrate a believer's humility **(2:27–28, 30)?** How does this relate to **2:10–11?** What other biblical character also displayed humility in similar circumstances **(Genesis 41:16)?**

3. To what does the expression "days to come," perhaps better translated "latter days," **(2:28)** refer **(Genesis 49:1, 10; Numbers 24:14, 17; Isaiah 2:2–4; Hosea 3:5; Hebrews 1:1–2; 1 John 2:18)**?

The Dream Related

Read **Daniel 2:31–35.**

1. What would be the implication of the fact that each successive part of the image was composed of a less valuable metal than the previous section?

2. What is said about the stone that distinguishes it from the carefully crafted image seen in the dream **(2:34)**?

3. What part of the image was struck by the stone? What happened to the entire image as a result? What does this indicate?

The Dream Interpreted

Read **Daniel 2:36–45.**

1. Is there any evidence that Daniel's three friends were still with him at this point **(2:36)**?

2. How did Daniel's interpretation indicate that the God of Judah was involved even in the accomplishments of the kingdoms of the earth (**2:37–38**)?

3. There are at least three differences between the kingdoms represented by the image and that symbolized by the stone. What are these differences?

4. How did Nebuchadnezzar's dream teach the same things that are enunciated in the following passages from the New Testament: **Matthew 13:31–32; Mark 4:26–29; John 18:36; 1 Thessalonians 2:12; Hebrews 1:8; Hebrews 12:28; Revelation 11:15.**

5. In the light of all this, who is the one who came to establish God's kingdom?

The Aftermath of the Interpretation

Read **Daniel 2:46–49.**

1. What was Nebuchadnezzar's reaction to all of this? How does this relate to what was said in **2:6?**

2. What was Daniel's reaction and why was it appropriate **(2:49)**?

The Word for Us

1. What are some temptations that we face to choose the kingdoms of the world instead of the kingdom of God?

2. How does this chapter strengthen us to resist temptations to follow the world rather than Christ?

Closing

Sing or read together the following stanza of "Glorious Things of You Are Spoken":

> Glorious things of you are spoken,
> Zion, city of our God;
> He whose word cannot be broken
> Formed you for His own abode.
> On the Rock of Ages founded,
> What can shake your sure repose?
> With salvation's walls surrounded,
> You may smile at all your foes.

Lesson 4

The Three Men
in the Fiery Furnace

Theme Verse

"If we are thrown into the blazing furnace, the God we serve is able to save us from it, and He will rescue us from your hand, O king. But even if He does not, we want you to know, O king, that we will not serve your gods or worship the image of gold you have set up." (**Daniel 3:17–18**)

Goal

The goal of this lesson is that we may more firmly believe that no power on earth can imperil us since we are in the care and protection of our heavenly Father.

What's Going On Here?

Carried away by visions of his own greatness, Nebuchadnezzar erects a statue and summons officials from throughout his realm to show their complete allegiance to him by worshiping the statue. Shadrach, Meshach, and Abednego, however, have a higher allegiance. This chapter records the faithfulness of these men to their God and His miraculous faithfulness to them.

Searching the Scriptures

Nebuchadnezzar's Golden Image

Read **Daniel 3:1–7.**

1. What, perhaps, gave Nebuchadnezzar the idea for making this image

of gold **(Daniel 2:36–38)**?

2. Does the language of **3:1** mean that the image was made entirely of gold? Compare **Exodus 39:38; 40:5** with **37:25–26.** See also **Isaiah 40:19; 41:7; Jeremiah 10:3–4.**

A site known by the name Dura has been discovered by archaeologists. At this site there is a huge mound that might have served as the pedestal of the colossal image described in this chapter. The height of the statue given in **Daniel 3:1** may well include the measurement of such a pedestal.

3. What does **Daniel 3:5** say about the posture for worship often assumed in the ancient Near East? What does such a position say about the attitude of the worshiper toward the one who is worshiped?

4. Compare **3:6** with **Jeremiah 29:20–22.** What does this tell us about Nebuchadnezzar?

The Accusation against the Three Judeans
Read **Daniel 3:8–12.**

1. The wording of **verse 8** indicates that the three Judeans were maliciously accused or denounced. Seeing that the charges against them were in fact true, in what sense were the charges malicious?

2. What would have been involved in obeying Nebuchadnezzar's command **(3:12)**? Therefore, how is this situation similar to that recorded in **chapter 1?**

3. Of what are the three men charged (**3:12;** see also **2:49**)?

The King Confronts the Three Young Men
Read **Daniel 3:13–18.**
1. What was the result of the malicious accusations of the Chaldeans **(3:13)**?

2. What was Nebuchadnezzar's offer to the three men **(3:14–15)**? Why might he have given them this second chance?

3. What role do the words at the end of **verse 15** play in the overall story?

4. How are we to understand the words in **3:17–18** ("the God we serve is able ... But even if He does not, ...")? What was remarkable about the faith of the three young men? How was their answer an illustration of the

kind of life Jesus described in **Mark 8:34–38?** How is it an illustration of what is said in **Acts 14:21–22; 2 Timothy 3:12;** and **2 Corinthians 12:7–10?**

The Punishment Is Increased

Read **Daniel 3:19–23.**

1. What indicated the greatness of Nebuchadnezzar's anger toward the three young men?

2. What indications are there of the severity of the punishment that was inflicted on the Judeans?

3. What item of information is given in **3:23** that shows both the utter helplessness of the three men and the wonder of the miracle that follows?

The Miraculous Deliverance

Read **Daniel 3:24–27.**

1. In the Greek translations of Daniel there occurs a lengthy addition between **verses 23** and **24.** This insertion consists largely of two canticles or prayers. A version of the latter of these is given in some hymnals (*Lutheran Worship* 9; *The Lutheran Hymnal*, page 120, "The Song of the Three Children"). Read through this canticle. Why would the Greek trans-

lators have felt it appropriate to include a hymn at this point?

2. What indications that a miraculous deliverance had taken place are mentioned in **3:25?** Who was the fourth figure seen by Nebuchadnezzar? Compare verses **25** and **28**.

3. What confession was made by the king **(3:26)?** Do you think it was a confession of faith in the God of Judah as the only true God?

4. What further evidences of the extent of the miracle are given in **3:27?** Who confirmed that the miracle had taken place?

Nebuchadnezzar's Decree

Read **Daniel 3:28–30.**

1. What did the king state about the three young men and their God in **3:28?** How would you relate what is said in this verse about the three to **Hebrews 11:32–34** (especially **verse 34**)?

2. What did Nebuchadnezzar acknowledge about the God of the three men (**3:29**)? What did he threaten to do to those who spoke anything against their God (compare **3:29** and **2:5**)?

3. In light of **2:49** what did the king do for the three young men according to **3:30**?

The Word for Us

1. The Aramaic of **Daniel 3:8** literally says that their opponents "devoured the pieces of" the Judeans. Note the similar language used in **Galatians 5:15.** How do these two portions of Scripture depict the destructive potential of malicious speech?

2. What encouragement and guidance does this chapter give to believers who face suffering (for example, one whose friends are pressuring him to do something wrong or one whose employer wants her to do something dishonest or even illegal)?

3. How does **1 Peter 4:12–19** develop the themes of this chapter, and what encouragement does it give believers who are suffering for their Christian faith?

Closing

Sing or read together "All You Works of the Lord."

1. All you works of the Lord, bless the Lord—praise Him and magnify Him forever.
2. You angels of the Lord, bless the Lord; you heavens, bless the Lord;
3. all you powers of the Lord, bless the Lord—praise Him and magnify Him forever.
4. You sun and moon, bless the Lord; you stars of heaven, bless the Lord;
5. you showers and dew, bless the Lord—praise Him and magnify Him forever.
6. You winds of God, bless the Lord; you fire and heat, bless the Lord;
7. you winter and summer, bless the Lord—praise Him and magnify Him forever.
8. You dews and frost, bless the Lord; you frost and cold, bless the Lord;
9. you ice and snow, bless the Lord—praise Him and magnify Him forever.
10. You nights and days, bless the Lord; you light and darkness, bless the Lord;
11. you lightnings and clouds, bless the Lord—praise Him and magnify Him forever.
12. Let the earth bless the Lord; you mountains and hills, bless the Lord;
13. all you green things that grow on the earth, bless the Lord—praise Him and magnify Him forever.
14. You wells and springs, bless the Lord; you rivers and seas, bless the Lord;
15. you whales and all who move in the waters, bless the Lord—praise Him and magnify Him forever.
16. All you birds of the air, bless the Lord; all you beasts and cattle, bless the Lord;
17. all you children of mortals, bless the Lord—praise Him and magnify Him forever.
18. You people of God, bless the Lord; you priests of the Lord, bless the Lord;
19. you servants of the Lord, bless the Lord—praise Him and magnify Him forever.
20. You spirits and souls of the righteous, bless the Lord; you pure and humble of heart, bless the Lord;
21. let us bless the Father and the Son and the Holy Spirit—praise Him and magnify Him forever.
22. Glory be to the Father and to the Son and to the Holy Spirit;
23. as it was in the beginning, is now, and will be forever. Amen.

(Text © 1978. By permission of CPH.)

Lesson 5

Nebuchadnezzar's Madness

Theme Verse

"Now I, Nebuchadnezzar, praise and exalt and glorify the King of heaven, because everything He does is right and all His ways are just. And those who walk in pride He is able to humble." **(Daniel 4:37)**

Goal

The goal of this lesson is that we may be moved to greater humility in view of the majesty and mercy of God, which surpass all understanding.

What's Going On Here?

The great Nebuchadnezzar ruled much of the known world and built magnificent buildings in a glorious city. The arrogant Nebuchadnezzar attributed his achievements to his own power and thought they were all to serve his majesty. To this Nebuchadnezzar the Lord gave a troubling dream and caused that dream to come true in order that the great and arrogant Nebuchadnezzar (along with all the living) would learn "that the Most High is sovereign over the kingdoms of men and gives them to anyone He wishes and sets over them the lowliest of men" **(Daniel 4:17).**

Searching the Scriptures

The Edict of Nebuchadnezzar

Read **Daniel 4:1–3.**

1. What impression is given in **4:1** regarding the importance Nebuchadnezzar attached to what he was going to relate? What does this verse illus-

trate about Nebuchadnezzar (and indeed all the Babylonian kings)?

The king is eager to relate the "miraculous signs and wonders" that the Most High performed on him. These words indicate that the chapter deals with events that were quite out of the ordinary.

2. How much would Nebuchadnezzar acknowledge about the Most High God (**4:2–3**)? Do you think this is evidence of saving faith on his part (compare **4:8, 18**)?

Nebuchadnezzar's Dream

Read **Daniel 4:4–8.**

1. What does **4:4** indicate about the king's status at the time when he experienced this dream? How would you relate this to the overall message of the chapter?

2. In light of the events recorded in **chapter 2,** why might Nebuchadnezzar have summoned Daniel only after his other wise men had been unable to give him an interpretation (**1 Kings 22:5–9**)?

The Content of the Dream

Read **Daniel 4:9–18.**

1. What similarities do you find between **4:9** and **Ezekiel 28:3**?

2. What is the meaning of the description of the tree of Nebuchadnez-zar's dream **(4:10–12; Ezekiel 17:22–24; 31:1–11, 18; Mark 4:30–32)**? With whom is the tree to be identified **(4:22)**?

3. Who were the watchers (see NIV text note) and holy ones mentioned in **4:13, 17**? What hymn makes use of these names?

4. To what might the iron and bronze refer **(4:15)**?

Reread **4:16**. "Seven" is probably used here as a number of complete-ness, meaning that these things will take place until the purpose for their happening has been completed, rather than having reference to any specif-ic measure of time (such as seven years). The term rendered "mind" in many translations of this verse is the term commonly rendered "heart" (as it is in the King James Version). This word is used in the Scriptures to refer to the entire inner life of a person, reason as well as emotions and spiritual condition **(Deuteronomy 4:29; 1 Samuel 16:7; Job 1:5; Jeremiah 31:33)**.

5. What is the meaning of **4:17**? See **4:24**.

Daniel's Interpretation and Advice

Read **Daniel 4:19–27**.

1. Compare **4:25** and **4:17**. For whom is the message of the dream and its interpretation intended?

2. Compare **4:26** and **4:32**. What is the meaning of the word *heaven* in **4:26**? Where else in Scripture is this term used in this way? Compare **Matthew 8:11** with **Luke 13:29**.

3. What is the meaning of **4:27**?

Nebuchadnezzar's Madness

Read **Daniel 4:28–33.** According to Nebuchadnezzar's statement in **4:30,** how seriously did he take the message of the dream and Daniel's advice?

The medical term for the disease that afflicted the king is boanthropy. This is a malady in which one conducts himself or herself as though he or she were an ox or cow, subsisting entirely on grass. Although this disease is extremely rare, it has been observed in modern times. A Babylonian inscription from Nebuchadnezzar's reign probably makes reference to his madness. Further information is given in *Introduction to the Old Testament,* by Roland K. Harrison (Grand Rapids: Eerdmans, 1969), pp. 1114–17 or *The Interpreter's Dictionary of the Bible* (Nashville: Abingdon, 1962), vol. 1, p. 851 and vol. 3, pp. 220–21.

Nebuchadnezzar's Recovery

Read **Daniel 4:34–37.**
1. What is the relationship between the two events recorded in **4:34**?

2. According to **4:35** who is beyond God's control?

The advisors and nobles mentioned in **4:36** had probably conducted the affairs of the king's government during the time of his madness.

3. What happened to Nebuchadnezzar after his reason returned to him **(4:36–37)**? What other biblical character underwent a similar change of heart with respect to the Lord **(1 Kings 21:25–29)**?

The Word for Us

1. What are other examples of people who exhibited such pride? How does their life illustrate the truth that God will bring low the proud, if not in this life, then in the one to come?

2. Read **Philippians 2:5–11. Verse 5** reads, "Have among yourselves this mind [of humility], which you have [when you are] in Christ Jesus" (author's translation). To be "in Christ Jesus" is to be in a relationship with Jesus Christ through faith in Him **(Galatians 3:14, 26; 5:6; Colossians 2:6–7).** This relationship of faith is created and sustained by Baptism **(Galatians 3:26–27; Romans 6:3–4, 11)** and the Gospel **(1 Corinthians 4:15, 17; Ephesians 1:13; 3:6).** How, therefore, may one have a mind of humility?

3. Compare **Philippians 2:3–4** with **1 Corinthians 13:4–5;** see also **Philippians 2:1–2.** What does this tell us about the relationship of humility and love? What insight does this give you into showing love toward other people?

Closing

Sing or read together "Come Down, O Love Divine":

Come down, O Love divine;
Seek out this soul of mine,
And visit it with Your own ardor glowing;
O Comforter, draw near;
Within my heart appear,
And kindle it, Your holy flame bestowing.

Oh, let it freely burn
Till worldly passions turn
To dust and ashes in its heat consuming;
And let Your glorious light
Shine ever on my sight
And clothe me round, the while my path illuming.

Let holy charity
My outward vesture be
And lowliness become my inner clothing—
True lowliness of heart,
Which takes the humbler part
And over its shortcomings weeps with loathing.

And so the yearning strong,
With which the soul will long,
Shall far outpass the pow'r of human telling;
No soul can guess His grace
Till it become the place
Wherein the Holy Spirit makes His dwelling.

Lesson 6

A Feast and a Den of Lions

Theme Verse

"He is the living God and He endures forever; His kingdom will not be destroyed, His dominion will never end. He rescues and He saves; He performs signs and wonders in the heavens and on the earth. He has rescued Daniel from the power of the lions." **(Daniel 6:26–27)**

Goal

The lesson aims to teach us that in spite of the insolence of the unbelieving world and the manner in which it oppresses the people of God, we may rely completely on the grace and goodness of our God.

What's Going On Here?

This lesson covers two narratives from the book of Daniel. In the first we see the pride of another Babylonian ruler and how the Lord humbled him. In the second we see another of God's faithful people in a desperate situation, one from which his faithful Lord rescued him.

Searching the Scriptures

Belshazzar's Feast

Read **Daniel 5:1–4.**

There has been much debate among scholars about the use of the term *king* for Belshazzar and the description of Nebuchadnezzar as his father. As you have time and interest, consult the background information about these issues in the leaders notes.

How would you characterize the way Belshazzar and his guests used the temple vessels **(5:2–4)**?

The Handwriting on the Wall

Read **Daniel 5:5–12.**

The palace mentioned in this chapter has been unearthed by archaeologists. The walls were covered with plaster, just as is described in passing in **Daniel 5:5.**

1. Why might Belshazzar have only offered to make the one who could read the handwriting on the wall the third ruler in the land **(5:7)**? See the background information in the leaders notes of the previous section.

2. Who might the "queen" **(5:10)** have been? Compare **5:2**.

Daniel's Summoning and Interpretation

Read **Daniel 5:13–28.**

1. What are we to make of Daniel's refusal of the king's gifts **(5:17)**? What other man of God acted in a similar way in similar circumstances **(2 Kings 5:8–16)**?

2. What did Daniel note about the power Nebuchadnezzar possessed in terms of both its extent **(5:18–19)** and its source **(5:21)**? What should Belshazzar have learned from Nebuchadnezzar's experience? What did he do instead?

3. What contrast is drawn in Daniel's speech between the true God and all other gods (5:23)? See also the following references, where a similar contrast is drawn: **Deuteronomy 4:28; Psalm 115:3–8; 135:15–18; Isaiah 44:9–20.** What do the last three passages say about those who worship such gods?

4. What interpretation does Daniel offer for the handwriting on the wall (5:26–28)?

The Aftermath
Read **Daniel 5:29–31.** What took place that very night (5:30)?

Darius the Mede is unknown to us from any other source. Many scholars believe that he is to be identified with one who is known otherwise as Gobryas of Gutium, who was a "righthand man" to Cyrus. Apparently Cyrus entrusted the rule of the ancient kingdom of the Chaldeans (the area around Babylon and not the entire empire of Nebuchadnezzar) to this man. Such an identification would fit with **Daniel 5:31,** which can more literally be translated "Darius the Mede received the kingdom" and **9:1,** which says of Darius that he was "made ruler over the Babylonian [Chaldean] kingdom." It is argued that Darius' age is noted in **5:31** as a way of indicating that his rule was a brief one.

Others argue that Darius is to be identified with Cyrus himself, who was about 60 years old when he conquered Babylon. These scholars argue that **Daniel 6:28** should be translated, "… the reign of Darius, that is, the reign of Cyrus." See NIV text note.

The Plot against Daniel
Read **Daniel 6:1–8.**
1. What did Darius do to improve the administration of his kingdom

(6:1–2)?

2. Why did Daniel fare so well in the administration of this new government **(6:3–4)?** See also **5:12, 14.**

3. What was false about what was told to Darius by those who were plotting against Daniel **(6:7)?** What decree did they propose that the king issue? What motivated their request **(6:3–5)?**

4. What was unique about such decrees under the law of the Medes and Persians **(6:8)?** See also **Esther 1:19; 8:8.**

The Consequences of Daniel's Courage
Read **Daniel 6:9–18.**

1. Where did Daniel pray (**6:10;** see **Acts 10:9**), and what would have been the result of his action? When did he pray (compare **Psalm 55:17**)? Considering the danger that he was in, what was remarkable about the content of his prayers?

2. Even though Daniel was a loyal servant of the government, he disobeyed this direct order of his king. How is his action an illustration of

Acts 5:29? What does this contribute to our understanding of a believer's responsibility toward the state as we have identified it in previous lessons?

3. What charge and innuendo were raised against Daniel **(6:13)?**

Daniel in the Lions' Den
Read **Daniel 6:19–24.**

1. How are we to understand the word *innocent* (rendered "blameless" in some translations) in **6:22?** What does this verse tell us about God's angels?

2. Why was Daniel delivered from the lions **(6:23; Hebrews 11:33)?**

3. What is the meaning of **6:24?**

The Decree of the King
Read **Daniel 6:25–28.**

1. What did the decree of Darius require of the people under his jurisdiction **(6:26)?** Compare **5:19.**

2. How did the consequences of Daniel's action turn out to be the opposite of what was planned for him by his opponents **(6:28)**?

The Word for Us

1. Read **Revelation 18:2–4** and **21:1–4** in light of **Daniel 5.** How do these portions of Scripture encourage us while living in this evil and often hostile world?

2. Relate **Daniel 6** to **Matthew 10:24–33.** How are Christians today called on to confess Christ?

3. How would you relate the message of **1 Peter 2:21–25** and **3:17–18** to the encouragement offered by **Daniel 6?**

4. How would these two chapters offer encouragement to Christians who are suffering for their faith, particularly those who are suffering at the hands of a hostile government?

Closing

Sing or read together the following stanzas of "If God Himself Be for Me":

If God Himself be for me,
I may a host defy;
For when I pray, before me
My foes, confounded, fly.
If Christ, my head and master,
Befriend me from above,
What foe or what disaster
Can drive me from His love?

I build on this foundation,
That Jesus and His blood
Alone are my salvation,
The true, eternal good.
Without Him all that pleases
Will vain and empty prove.
The gifts I have from Jesus
Alone are worth my love.

No angel and no gladness,
No high place, pomp, or show,
No love, no hate, no badness,
No sadness, pain, or woe,
No scheming, no contrivance,
No subtle thing or great
Shall draw me from Your guidance
Nor from You separate.

For joy my heart is ringing;
All sorrow disappears;
And full of mirth and singing,
It wipes away all tears.
The sun that cheers my spirit
Is Jesus Christ, my king;
The heav'n I shall inherit
Makes me rejoice and sing.

Lesson 7

The Son of Man

Theme Verse

"In my vision at night I looked, and there before me was one like a son of man, coming with the clouds of heaven. He approached the Ancient of Days and was led into His presence. He was given authority, glory and sovereign power; all peoples, nations and men of every language worshiped Him. His dominion is an everlasting dominion that will not pass away, and His kingdom is one that will never be destroyed." **(Daniel 7:13–14)**

Goal

The goal of this lesson is that we may be strengthened in our faith in Christ as we see all that He has done, is doing, and will do for us as Son of Man and Son of God.

What's Going On Here?

In spite of its difficulties the seventh chapter of Daniel is one of the most meaningful in all the Old Testament. For this reason we will devote the next two sessions to it. We will do so under two headings: the Son of Man (the topic of this lesson) and the kingdom of God.

Searching the Scriptures
Daniel's Dream and Visions

Read **Daniel 7:1–28.**

1. What is the purpose of mentioning the four winds of heaven (**7:2;**

Zechariah 2:6; 6:5 [see NIV text note])?

2. What is the significance of the fact that the four beasts of this chapter are said to arise from the sea **(7:2–3; Psalm 78:13–14; Isaiah 17:12–13; 57:20; Jeremiah 47:2)?** In this light what is the meaning of **Revelation 21:1?** What do the beasts of **Daniel 7:2** symbolize **(7:17)?**

3. Who is represented by the figure described in **7:9?** What is indicated by the name *the Ancient of Days?* What is the significance of the description of His clothing and hair as being pure white **(Psalm 51:7; Isaiah 1:18)?**

4. With what natural phenomenon did Daniel see the "one like a son of man" **(7:13)?** What does this mean, seeing that the four beasts arose from the sea **(Psalm 104:1–3)?** What is the significance of the fact that this figure is called "one like a son of man" in contrast to those who are symbolized by beasts?

5. What is said to have been given to this one like a son of man **(7:14)?** What is He said to have received from people? How is what is said here echoed in **Revelation 5:12–13?** The extent and duration of that which is given to Him is also mentioned in **Daniel 7:14** and in **7:27.** What is the extent and duration of that which is possessed by the one like a son of man and the Ancient of Days?

6. Who also received sovereignty, power, and kingdom **(7:18, 27)?** See also **1 Corinthians 3:21–23**. With whom are we to identify these? See, for example, **1 Corinthians 1:2**. How is it that these things can be given to this group of people as well as to the individual who is called one like a son of man? See **Acts 9:4–5**. Compare **1 Corinthians 1:30** with **2 Corinthians 5:21**.

7. How does the duration of the kingdom of the one like a son of man and the saints of the Most High **(Daniel 7:14, 18, 27)** compare with that which is symbolized by the four beasts **(7:11–12)?**

Jesus' Use of the Title *Son of Man*

The term *Son of man* was our Lord's favorite way of referring to Himself. He used this term as a way of identifying Himself as the figure spoken of in **Daniel 7:13–14.** However, He also gave this title a great deal of added meaning, for He used it in a number of different ways to refer to several aspects of His person and work. Although Jesus could employ this term simply as a roundabout way of saying "I," He most often used it with reference to one or more of the following:

1. *The Second Coming*—The immediate reference to the one like a son of man in **Daniel 7** is to His "coming with the clouds of the heaven" for judgment. Our Lord often used this term when speaking of His final return in judgment.

2. *Equality with God*—In **Daniel 7** this one like a son of man appears as an equal with the Ancient of Days. Jesus sometimes used this title for Himself when referring to His status as God from all eternity. Later in this lesson we will see how this is developed in **Revelation.**

3. *Divine authority*—Related to point 2 is our Lord's assertions of His divine authority. Therefore we are not surprised to see that He called Himself the Son of man when declaring that He was Lord of the Sabbath and that He had authority to forgive sins.

4. *Messianic King*—The reference in **Daniel 7** to thrones of judgment gives a royal air to the picture of the Son of man. A royal theme is important for the Old Testament, for the promised Savior (known by New Testament times as the Messiah and the one who was *coming*) was to be a king from David's line (see **2 Samuel 7:11b–16** and **Luke 1:31–33**). Since the term *Messiah* was heard by many people in our Lord's day to be a call to armed rebellion against the Romans **(Luke 23:2),** Jesus much preferred to assert that He was the promised messianic King by use of the title *Son of man* rather than that of *Messiah* (for which the Greek equivalent is "Christ").

5. *Humility*—The original meaning of the term *son of man* was "human being" and denoted man as being far below the exalted status of God. The term is so used in **Psalm 8:3–5; Daniel 8:17;** and throughout **Ezekiel.** Our Lord, therefore, also used this title when speaking of His state of humiliation and the lowly circumstances in which He lived while He was here on this earth.

6. *Passion predictions*—The most famous use of the title *Son of man* by Jesus occurs in His various predictions of His suffering, death, and resurrection. In these He combined Daniel's description of the Son of man with Isaiah's portrait of the Servant of the Lord. This is given its most thorough presentation in **Isaiah 52:13–53:12.**

7. *Reveals God*—In speaking of Himself as the only one who was able to reveal God the Father to humanity, our Lord also employed the title *Son of Man.* In so doing, He was combining Daniel's description with one of the earliest messianic prophecies in all the Old Testament, namely, that of the prophet like Moses, which is recorded in **Deuteronomy 18:15–18.** In these "Son of man" passages, there is often an emphasis on the word as that through which the Son of man reveals God and His workings to people.

Look up the following passages in which Jesus used the term *Son of man*. Match each passage with the use of the phrase described in the preceding paragraphs that best expresses the meaning of the passage.

Matthew 8:20   **Matthew 12:40**

Matthew 13:37   **Matthew 16:28**
(in light of **Mark 4:14**)   (a prediction of the Transfiguration)

Mark 2:10   **Mark 8:31**

Mark 10:45   Mark 14:62

Luke 6:5   Luke 12:40

Luke 19:10   John 1:51

John 6:62   John 12:23, 32, 34

A Scene of Judgment

1. Who are the "thousands upon thousands" and "ten thousand times ten thousand" (**Daniel 7:10**) who attend the Ancient of Days (**Deuteronomy 33:2; Revelation 5:11**)? How does this relate to Jesus' use of "Son of man" (**Matthew 25:31**)?

2. What is the purpose of this assembly (**Daniel 7:10, 22, 26**)? What, therefore, is represented by the books mentioned in **Daniel 7:10** (**Malachi 3:16; Luke 10:20; Revelation 20:12**)?

3. When the judgment is rendered, against whom is it given (**Daniel 7:11–12, 26**)? In whose favor is it given (**Daniel 7:22, 27**)? How would you relate what is said here to the biblical doctrine of justification (**Romans 4:3, 5, 22–25; 5:18–19**)?

The Word for Us

1. What is the significance of the term *Son of man* containing elements of both lowliness (humility, prediction of suffering and death) and exaltedness (resurrection, equality with God, Second Coming)?

2. Some in Jesus' day longed for Him to be a provider of the good they desired but rejected Him when He presented the true meaning of His ministry **(John 6).** Also today some would present Jesus and the Christian faith as the way to gain what is desirable while minimizing, ignoring, or even denying elements of Christ's ministry and teaching that they do not find agreeable. How would the material we have studied in this lesson speak to this?

3. What guidance does this portion of Scripture supply for us in choosing proper values and in setting right priorities in life?

4. How would the material we have studied in this lesson strengthen a Christian as he or she struggles with those things that compete against Jesus Christ for allegiance?

Closing

Read together the hymns of praise from **Revelation 5:9–10, 12–13.**

Lesson 8

God's Kingdom
and World Kingdoms

Theme Verse

"Then the sovereignty, power and greatness of the kingdoms under the whole heaven will be handed over to the saints, the people of the Most High. His kingdom will be an everlasting kingdom, and all rulers will worship and obey Him." **(Daniel 7:27)**

Goal

The goal of this lesson is that we may understand what the Scriptures mean when they describe the kingdom of God, so that we may be encouraged to greater faith as we live among the kingdoms of this world.

What's Going On Here?

In our last session we studied **Daniel 7** from the point of what was said there with respect to the "Son of man," which played such a major role in the ministry and teaching of Jesus. During this session we will again devote our attention to **Daniel 7,** one of the richest chapters in all the Old Testament. This time we will study the chapter in light of the distinctions it draws between the kingdom of God and the kingdoms of the world.

Searching the Scriptures

The Four World Empires

Reread **Daniel 7.** The beasts of **Daniel 7** are symbols of four extensive empires **(7:17).** As was the case with Nebuchadnezzar's dream in **chapter 2,** these four empires are representative of all the kingdoms of the world as they are set in opposition to the kingdom of God. Thus the dream of **chapter 7** proclaims the victory of the kingdom of the Son of Man over the kingdoms of the world **(7:14, 27)**.

1. How is the appearance of the first beast described **(7:4)**? With what specific kingdom is it possible to identify this beast **(Jeremiah 50:17; Ezekiel 17:3, 12)**? Daniel adds that this beast was raised up on its feet like a man and was given the heart of a man (in biblical vocabulary the "heart" refers to the seat of the intellect as well as to the emotions). How is this a confirmation of the identification of this beast with a particular world empire **(Daniel 4:33–36)**?

2. In what way is the appearance of the next two beasts described **(7:5–6)**? Compare **Daniel 7:5–6** with **Daniel 8:20–22.** With what two empires are these two beasts to be identified? In this light what is the significance of the remark that the second beast was raised up on one side? Today many scholars claim that the author of **Daniel** intended to say that the third beast symbolizes the empire of the Persians and that the second beast represents a separate empire of the Medes. Does this seem possible in light of **Daniel 8:20; 5:28;** and **6:8, 12?**

3. What evidence is there that the fourth beast of **Daniel 7:7** symbolizes the same kingdom as the fourth kingdom of **Daniel 2 (2:40)**? In view of what is said in **Daniel 2:44–45,** what empire is symbolized by the fourth beast of **Daniel 7?**

4. **Daniel 7:11–12** describes the overthrow of the four world empires. What, therefore, is the significance of the date given at the beginning of this chapter **(7:1)**?

5. What is the origin of the kingdoms of the four world empires (**7:17**)? What is different about the kingdom of the one like a son of man (**7:13**)? See also **John 18:36**.

6. Out of the last world empire there arises another "kingdom" symbolized by the little horn. What sort of a "reign" does the horn have in relationship to the people of God (**7:21, 25**)? What does **7:23** suggest about conditions for God's people prior to the end of the world? See also **Matthew 24:3–14, 29–31**. How does the vision indicate that the reign of this little horn is a lot of talk that ultimately cannot be backed up (**7:8, 11, 26**)? How should we relate this last passage (and indeed the entire chapter) to **Revelation 13:1–8?** What would the round number 10 suggest is meant by the symbolism of the 10 horns?

Note that the length of time that the little horn will oppress the saints of the Most High is given as "time, times and half a time" (**7:25**). Some add up the "times" as follows: a time plus two times plus half a time. The resulting three and a half times is half of the number seven, which symbolizes completeness. The meaning would thus be that Antichrist and the powers of this world will prevail over the people of God for only a limited time, until the Lord intervenes on their behalf (on the Last Day). Another possible explanation of this phrase is that the little horn has power at the beginning (time), after which his power and success doubles (times), but only with the result that his power is vastly diminished (half a time).

Whatever the interpretation of this particular phrase, the message of the entire chapter is that such opposition will not go on forever. What will last forever are blessings for those who put their trust in the one like a son of man. This is especially meaningful for the readers of Daniel who are experiencing oppression and difficulty for their faith.

7. Who gives Daniel the meaning of his vision (**7:16**)? See also **8:16–17;**

9:21–22. What comfort can we derive from Daniel's comments in **7:15** and **28?**

8. How is the deliverance of God's people described **(7:22)?** By comparing **7:13–14** with **7:22** through whom can we say that this deliverance is accomplished?

The Kingdom of God

Daniel 7 draws a contrast between the kingdoms of this world and the kingdom of God. Like the title "Son of man" the expression "the kingdom of God" (or "the kingdom of heaven") played a most significant role in the teaching of Jesus. This being the case, it will be helpful for us to examine some of what the New Testament has to say about this concept. In so doing we will note many similarities between Jesus' use of the title "Son of man" (as we looked at in the previous lesson) and the way in which He employed the phrase "kingdom of God."

God's grace—When Jesus used the expression "the kingdom of God," He was referring to everything that God, for the sake of Christ, has done, does, and will do to reestablish His rule of grace in, over, and among people. "In" because the kingdom is not an external matter but one of faith; "over" because it is the work of God not people; "among" because God's rule of grace was accomplished among us by Christ and continues to be among us through His Word and sacraments. The kingdom of God came with the coming of Jesus Himself, since He Himself is God (as He indicated with His use of the title "Son of man"), and He came to give to all people God's kingdom of grace, although not all will receive it.

1. How are these truths expressed in **Luke 11:20** and **12:32?** According to **Daniel 7:22** who receives the kingdom?

Messianic king—The Old Testament promised a king from David's line, and in time this king came to be known as the Messiah. At times our Lord used the title "Son of man" to indicate that He was this promised Messiah. Thus the kingdom of God is set up by God's Messiah, who is Jesus.

2. How is this stated in **Luke 1:31–33?**

Authority to forgive—Our Lord called Himself the Son of man when indicating that He had the power to forgive sins. Through the forgiveness of sins Jesus gave people God's kingdom of grace.

3. How does **Matthew 16:18–19** demonstrate this?

Passion of Christ—Jesus spoke of Himself as the Son of man when foretelling His suffering, death, and resurrection.

4. How does the parable of the unjust stewards **(Matthew 21:33–43)** show the connection that exists between our Lord's passion and the establishment of the kingdom of God?

Humility—The title "Son of man" lent itself to describing the great humility Jesus endured, both His humility during His life on earth and His humility in dying on a cross. When speaking of the kingdom of God, Christ also indicated that its beginnings are often in great humility.

5. How did our Lord indicate this fact in **Mark 4:30–32?** How is this taught in **Daniel 7?**

Reveals God—When speaking of how He had come to reveal God to humanity, Jesus sometimes referred to Himself as the Son of man. In His teaching on the kingdom of God, He also indicated that through the Word of God He reveals God to us.

6. How did He indicate this in **Mark 4:3–8, 13–20, 26–29?**

Community—When our Lord came into our world, He picked 12 disciples to be the beginning of a community of the redeemed among whom God's rule of grace would be reestablished. Note the references to this community in **Daniel 7:18, 22, 27.** This community would not be restricted to certain locales (as are the kingdoms of this world) but would include people from all nations.

7. How is the universal nature of this community of God's kingdom indicated in **7:14?** How is this truth expressed in **Matthew 13:33?**

Coming in judgment—**Daniel 7** speaks of the Son of man coming for judgment. Jesus used the title *Son of man* when speaking of His coming in judgment on the Last Day. Note **Matthew 24:30–31; 25:31–46** in addition to the references given in the previous lesson.

8. How does **Matthew 13:36–43** use the concept of the kingdom of God to proclaim the same message? Compare this parable with what is taught in **Daniel 7:11–12, 22, 26–27.**

The Word for Us

1. What are some significant differences between the kingdoms of the world and the kingdom of God?

2. What guidance does **Daniel 7** give to Christians about seeking the kingdom of God even while they live within the kingdoms of the world?

3. What encouragement for faith is there for God's people in the message of **Daniel 7** regarding the Son of man and the kingdom of God?

Closing

Sing or read together the following stanzas of "Hail to the Lord's Anointed":

Hail to the Lord's anointed,
Great David's greater Son!
Hail, in the time appointed,
His reign on earth begun!
He comes to break oppression,
To set the captive free,
To take away transgression
And rule in equity.

He comes with rescue speedy
To those who suffer wrong,
To help the poor and needy
And bid the weak be strong;
To give them songs for sighing,
Their darkness turn to light,
Whose souls, condemned and dying,
Were precious in His sight.

Kings shall fall down before Him
And gold and incense bring;
All nations shall adore Him,
His praise all people sing.
To Him shall prayer unceasing
And daily vows ascend;
His kingdom still increasing,
A kingdom without end.

Lesson 9

The Ram and the He-Goat

Theme Verse

"He will cause deceit to prosper, and he will consider himself superior. When they feel secure, he will destroy many and take his stand against the Prince of princes. Yet he will be destroyed, but not by human power." **(Daniel 8:25)**

Goal

The goal of this lesson is that we may see in God's rule of history both His power and His concern for His people.

What's Going On Here?

In the previous chapter of Daniel, the prophet was granted a vision foretelling the rise and fall of four world empires. In this chapter Daniel sees another vision, in which he is given a prophecy regarding the second and third empires of the previous vision. As we study the material of this vision, we will want to keep in mind its relationship to the preceding chapter.

Searching the Scriptures

The Circumstances of the Vision

Read **Daniel 8:1–14.**

1. What is the significance of the prophet's statement that when he experienced this vision, he found himself in Susa **(Esther 1:2–3)?**

2. In what sense was Daniel present in Susa? Compare **Ezekiel 8:3–4** and **Revelation 17:1–3** (especially **verse 3**).

3. Summarize the details of the vision.

4. How might **Daniel 8:13** be an illustration of the end of **1 Peter 1:12?**

The Vision Interpreted

Read **Daniel 8:15–25.**

1. What help was given to Daniel in interpreting his vision **(8:16)?** Whose was the voice that commanded that this help be given to him? Recall the other occasions when this angel played a major role as a messenger of God **(Luke 1:8–20, 26–38).**

2. Why did Daniel panic **(8:17)** and swoon into a deep sleep **(8:18)** at the approach of the one mentioned in **verse 16 (Judges 13:22)?** What does this say about humanity's condition? How is this character's response to Daniel's stupor **(8:18)** an illustration of **Hebrews 1:14?**

3. What was symbolized by the ram **(8:3, 20)?** What, therefore, is the meaning of the fact that the ram's horns were of unequal size and that the

longer of the two horns was the second to come up?

4. Note the directions that this ram charged **(8:4).** What is the meaning of the statement that no beast could stand before him?

5. Of what is the goat and the great horn between his eyes a symbol **(8:5, 21)**? Note the direction from which he came. Is this an accurate symbol? What is the significance of the statement that he came forth without touching the ground? How much of the earth did he cover, and what is symbolized by this statement? Note the emotion the goat displayed toward the ram **(8:6)** and what he did to the ram **(8:7).** To what historical development does this correspond?

Note the four horns that replaced the goat's great horn when the latter was broken **(8:8, 22).** After Alexander's death (at a relatively young age), there was a long struggle over who would succeed him. After about 20 years, the four divisions of Alexander's empire were ruled by the following: (1) Cassander was ruler of Macedonia and Greece. (2) Lysimachus ruled Asia Minor. (3) Ptolemy was king of Egypt. (4) Seleucus had mastery of Syria and the territory east of Syria. None of these kingdoms ever attained anything like the glory or strength of Alexander's empire.

For most of the time from 320 B.C. until 198 B.C., Ptolemy and his descendants had control over the land of Palestine. In 198 this control passed into the hands of the descendants of Seleucus. We hear more about these latter two empires in the remainder of the book of Daniel.

6. The one little horn that grew out of the four horns **(8:9, 23)** is symbolic of Antiochus the Fourth, also known as Antiochus Epiphanes, a successor of Seleucus and ruler of Syria. In his vision, Daniel saw the horn grow in power to the south and the east and toward the beautiful, or glori-

ous, land **(8:9).** To what does this last designation refer **(Ezekiel 20:6)?**

The apocryphal book 1 Maccabees reports how Antiochus waged war to the south against Egypt (1:16–24) and to the east against the city of Elymais, a part of the old Persian empire (3:31, 37; 6:1–4). His assaults against the people of Israel in the glorious land are foretold in the remainder of Daniel's vision.

7. What is the meaning of the statement that the little horn cast down and trampled on the host of heaven and the stars **(8:10, 24; Daniel 12:3; Exodus 7:4** ["divisions" = "hosts"]; **12:41** ["divisions" = "hosts"]; **Revelation 12:4)?**

8. Whom else does the little horn oppose **(8:11, 25)?** As a result, what does the little horn do with respect to the worship and religion of the people of God **(8:12)?**

The Comfort in the Vision

1. **Daniel 8:24–25** describes the great power of the little horn. Yet what message of comfort is given at the end of **verse 25?** How would the little horn be overcome?

2. Note the length of time the little horn would be successful in his endeavors **(8:14).** After converting this designation of time to years, consider the meaning of this statement.

3. We have seen that the vision of this chapter gives us a second look at two of the world empires mentioned in the previous chapter. According to **Daniel 8:17** and **19** is this the only subject of this vision, or does it have a fuller significance? If Daniel's second vision does have a fuller meaning, to what does it also refer?

4. How is the message of this chapter also contained in **Matthew 24:21–31?** According to this latter portion of Scripture, to whom or what should we look for our deliverance? How is this like the deliverance mentioned in **Daniel 8:25?**

The Conclusion of the Vision

Read **Daniel 8:26–27.**

The command to Daniel in **8:26** to "seal up the vision" does not mean to keep it a secret but to preserve it or keep it intact.

Compare Daniel's reaction to the vision **(8:27)** with the reaction of the disciples to Jesus' teaching in **Mark 9:31–32.**

The Word for Us

1. What encouragement for faith can we derive from this chapter for times when we face opposition or hardship on account of our Christian faith?

2. How are the kingdoms and governments of the world sometimes used for evil purposes? How may God provide deliverance in such cases?

3. How can current crises in our world help prepare Christians for the last, great crisis, the final judgment?

Closing

Sing or read together "In God, My Faithful God":

In God, my faithful God,
I trust when dark my road;
Great woes may overtake me,
Yet He will not forsake me.
It is His love that sends them;
At His best time He ends them.

My sins fill me with care,
Yet I will not despair.
I build on Christ, who loves me;
From this rock nothing moves me.
To Him I will surrender,
To Him, my soul's defender.

If death my portion be,
It brings great gain to me;
It speeds my life's endeavor
To live with Christ forever.
He gives me joy in sorrow,
Come death now or tomorrow.

"So be it," then, I say
With all my heart each day.
Dear Lord, we all adore You,
We sing for joy before You.
Guide us while here we wander
Until we praise You yonder.

Lesson 10

Daniel's Prayer

Theme Verse

"O Lord, listen! O Lord, forgive! O Lord, hear and act! For Your sake, O my God, do not delay, because Your city and Your people bear Your Name." **(Daniel 9:19)**

Goal

The goal of this lesson is that we may be led to imitate the example of Daniel by confessing our sins and turning to God for forgiveness and help.

What's Going On Here?

The Persians had taken control of Babylon. Mighty, arrogant Babylon had been destroyed just as God's prophets had foretold. Now Daniel was looking for the fulfillment of God's promise to bring His people back to their land. But the sin that caused the exile was still evident in the lives of God's people. Knowing this, Daniel turned in repentance to the Lord and cast himself and his people on their merciful God.

Searching the Scriptures

The Setting of the Prayer

Read **Daniel 9:1–3.**

1. Daniel gave the date as the first year of Darius the Mede. What have we learned about this person from our previous studies of Daniel (**5:31; 6:28**)?

2. What portion of the Old Testament was Daniel studying on the occasion recounted here (9:2; Jeremiah 25:11–12; 29:10)? What had God promised His people through the prophet? Does Daniel's study say anything about the attitude that we should have toward the Scriptures?

3. What three things accompanied the prayer of Daniel (9:3)? What is the meaning of Daniel's use of these (Nehemiah 9:1–2; Esther 4:1–3; Jonah 3:5–9)? Why were these in keeping with the prayer that Daniel was about to offer?

Daniel's Prayer: The Confession
Read **Daniel 9:4–14.**
1. Compare **Daniel 9:4** with **Exodus 20:5–6; 34:6–10.** On what basis did Daniel have courage to offer this prayer to God?

2. In **Daniel 9:5,** what did Daniel confess on behalf of the people?

3. What additional wrong is mentioned in **verses 6** and **10?**

4. How did Daniel indicate the universality of Israel's guilt (**Daniel 9:7–8**)? What does this say to those of us who may be tempted to feel that we are not as sinful as are many others? Who would be indicated by the expression "both near and far" (**9:7; Jeremiah 40:2–6**)?

5. What does **Daniel 9:9** indicate as the Israelites' only hope for deliverance from the punishment that the Lord had imposed on them?

6. How does **Daniel 9:11** describe the punishment of the exile? How does this relate to **Deuteronomy 28:15, 36–37, 41, 49–52?** How does the punishment, therefore, relate to Daniel's words in **verse 4** and to the concepts that are the background for his words?

7. What did the prophet confess as the ongoing sin of the people of Israel **(9:13)**?

8. Who do **verses 7** and **14** indicate was responsible for Israel's plight?

Daniel's Prayer: The Petition

Read **Daniel 9:15–19.**

1. On what basis did Daniel come to the Lord with his requests **(9:15)**? How does this verse, therefore, relate to what was said in **verse 4**? What are some of the things the Lord accomplished by His "mighty hand"? What does it mean that in this event He made a name for Himself **(Isaiah 63:11–14; Jeremiah 32:20)**?

Daniel described Jerusalem as God's "holy hill" **(9:16)**. Jerusalem was the holy mountain of the Lord, for on Jerusalem's Mount Zion God had chosen to dwell among people with forgiveness, thereby sanctifying them, or making them holy.

2. What did it mean when the prophet prayed that the Lord would take His wrath and anger away from Jerusalem and the people of Israel according to all His "righteous acts" **(Psalm 71:1–2; Romans 3:21–22, 26)**?

3. For what was Daniel asking the Lord in **9:17,** which, in a more word-for-word translation, reads, "Let your face shine" on the temple **(Numbers 6:25; Psalm 80:3)**? Why would he pray that this would be done for the Lord's sake **(Psalm 23:3; 1 John 2:12)**? For what specific thing was Daniel praying **(Jeremiah 29:10)**?

4. What did it mean that Jerusalem was the city called by the Lord's name **(9:18; Jeremiah 7:10–12, 14, 30; 32:34)**? According to **9:18,** why could Israel look for deliverance from God? See also **9:9.** How would you relate this to the New Testament statements on the way of salvation **(Titus 3:4–7; 1 Timothy 1:12–16)**?

5. In light of **Daniel 9:19,** what must the Lord do in order that Daniel's prayer might be answered and the Israelites returned to their homeland?

6. What does it mean when Daniel says that the people of Israel had the Lord's name called over them **(9:19; Numbers 6:22–27)**?

Gabriel's Arrival with the Lord's Answer

Read **Daniel 9:20–23.**

1. How quickly was Daniel's prayer answered **(9:20–21, 23)**? Relate what is said here to **Isaiah 65:24** and **Matthew 6:7–8.**

2. The prophet noted that the angel came to him at the time of the evening sacrifice **(9:21).** What was significant about this time of day **(Ezra 9:5–6; Psalm 141:2)?** What does this suggest as a guide for our own practice with respect to prayer?

3. What was the answer to Daniel's prayer **(9:22–23)?**

The Word for Us

1. How is Daniel's prayer like the confessions and prayers for mercy we use in our corporate worship?

2. How does this section of Scripture guide us in dealing with our guilt?

Closing

Sing or read together "To You, Omniscient Lord of All":

To You, omniscient Lord of all,
With grief and shame I humbly call;
I see my sins against You, Lord,
The sins of thought, of deed and word.
They press me sore; to You I flee:
O God, be merciful to me!

O Jesus, let Your precious blood
Be to my soul a cleansing flood.
Turn not, O Lord, Your guest away,
But grant that justified I may
Go to my house, at peace to be:
O God, be merciful to me!

Lesson 11

The Prophecy
of the 70 "Sevens"

Theme Verse

"Seventy 'sevens' are decreed concerning your people and your holy city to bring an end to rebellion, to seal up sin, and to atone for iniquity, to bring eternal righteousness, to seal up vision and prophecy, and to anoint a holy of holies." (**Daniel 9:24,** author's translation)

Goal

The goal of this lesson is that we may see Jesus Christ as the center of the Scriptures and of the history of our salvation.

What's Going On Here?

Gabriel was sent by God in response to Daniel's prayer to make known to him a vision concerning the future and the coming of God's Anointed One. That vision is the subject of this lesson.

Searching the Scriptures
The Prophecy in Overview

Read the author's translation of **Daniel 9:24–27:**

> [24]Seventy "sevens" are decreed concerning your people and your holy city to bring an end to rebellion, to seal up sin, and to atone for iniquity, to bring eternal righteousness, to seal up vision and prophecy, and to anoint a holy of holies. [25]Know and understand this: From the going forth of a command to return and to rebuild Jerusalem to an anointed one, a prince, there are seven "sevens," and in sixty-two "sevens" it will be restored and

rebuilt with plaza and moat but in distressful times. [26]After sixty-two "sevens" the anointed will be cut off and have no more. A people of the prince who will come will ransack the city and the holy place, but his end will be with a flood, and until the end there will be war; desolations are strictly determined. [27]He will make great a covenant for many for one "seven," and for half of the "seven" he will abolish sacrifice and offering. On the wing of abominations will be one who makes desolate, until destruction, which is determined, pours out on the one who makes desolate.

1. What characteristic features of apocalyptic literature are to be found in these verses? (See lesson 1.)

2. As we attempt to understand these verses, what clear biblical teaching must we always keep in mind **(Matthew 24:42)**?

Part of the difficulty in interpreting this passage lies in translating the Hebrew word rendered "sevens" in the translation above and in the NIV. This is the normal word for "weeks," but everyone is agreed that literal weeks, each made up of seven days, cannot be the meaning intended here. Some translators, including those of the RSV (in **9:24**), have opted to render this word "weeks of years." However, this is conjectural and more of an interpretation than a translation.

It is helpful to recall that the number seven is often used in the Scriptures as a number of completeness. When multiplied by 10, another number denoting completeness, it often serves in this way. The literal translation "sevens" emphasizes this symbolic significance.

Many, many different interpretations of these four verses have been suggested during the last 1,900 years. However, nearly all of them can be assigned to one of the following four types:

(A) Those who interpret the Scriptures through the use of the historical-critical method claim that the book of Daniel was written in or about 165 B.C. The beginning of the 70 "weeks of years" is said to be about 587 B.C. The seven weeks of years brings one to the edict of Cyrus in 538 B.C. (587 minus 49) allowing God's people to return to the land of Judah. Since the author made a mistake in his calculations, the 62 weeks of years terminates in 171 B.C. (538 minus 434 equals 104, an error of nearly 70 years!)

with the death of the last legitimate high priest. The last week of years is divided into two halves, the first marking the desecration of the Jerusalem temple by Antiochus Epiphanes in 167, the second concluding with the end of the world (which the author erroneously predicted would take place in 164). The passage, therefore, contains little more than "prophecy" after the fact. In previous lessons we have examined various problems with this whole approach to the book of Daniel. For anyone who acknowledges the Bible to be the authoritative Word of God, this interpretation, which we may call the liberal or critical interpretation, must be soundly rejected.

(B) Those who wish to make this passage agree with their understanding of Revelation 20, that is, those who wish to interpret this passage in harmony with a literal, 1,000-year reign of Christ and believers on earth prior to the end of the world, hold to the "gap" or "parenthesis" interpretation. These interpreters begin reckoning the 70 weeks of years at 445 B.C. (when Nehemiah returned to Jerusalem to complete the rebuilding of the city walls), so that the 69 weeks of years end with the ministry of Jesus. The last week foretells the seven-year period called the "tribulation," which falls between the "rapture" and the 1,000-year reign of Christ on earth. Thus it is said that there is a gap or parenthesis, now having lasted over 1,900 years, between the 69th and the 70th weeks. A full refutation of this view would require a class all to itself. Suffice it to say the following: (1) The 1,000 years of Revelation 20 are a symbol for the entire New Testament era. (2) There is no biblical evidence whatsoever for the "rapture" or a seven-year "tribulation." (3) 445 is hardly the most likely date for the beginning of the 70 "sevens" of this chapter. (4) 69 weeks of years after 445 B.C. would reach A.D. 38 (several years after the end of Jesus' earthly ministry. (5) It is highly subjective to insert an unmentioned "gap" into the vision's "timetable" of 70 "sevens." (6) **Matthew 24:42** has already warned us against trying to use this passage to calculate exact dates in the history of our salvation.

(C) A third interpretation may be styled the "traditional messianic" interpretation. This approach understands the 70 "sevens" as being nothing more exact than very approximate designations of time. According to this view, the 69th "seven" marks the death of Jesus. Since this understanding of the passage may be the correct one, we will examine it in greater detail during our study of the individual verses.

(D) A fourth interpretation of the passage in question is in essence very similar to the third and may be called the "typical messianic" or Christian church view. This understanding of these verses sees the "sevens" as specifying periods of time (which have been determined by God) without any indication of their duration. According to those who interpret the passage in this way the seven "sevens" mark the coming of Jesus, the 62 "sevens" symbolize the entire history of the Christian church, and the last "seven" describes a time just prior to the end of the world and Christ's second coming. On the whole, this understanding of the passage seems the most satisfactory, although there are points at which interpretation C seems to involve less difficulty. Therefore, we will expound this approach in much greater detail as we examine the passage verse by verse.

The Benefits of the Seventy "Sevens"

Reread **Daniel 9:24** in the translation given above.

1. In delivering the message of this vision to Daniel the angel Gabriel stated that the 70 "sevens" had been decreed concerning "your people and your holy city." To whom or what do these two expressions refer **(Revelation 21:2)?**

2. The angel listed six purposes of the 70 "sevens." The first three are apparently three different ways of describing the same thing. What terms are used in designating these three purposes? What important Old Testament ordinance lies in the background of what is promised in this part of the passage **(Leviticus 16:24–27, 29–30, 34)?** Therefore, how was this promise fulfilled (compare **Leviticus 16:27** with **Hebrews 13:11–12**)?

3. The first of the positive purposes mentioned refers to righteousness. What is said of this righteousness in this passage? How is righteousness accomplished **(2 Corinthians 5:21)?**

4. What is the fifth purpose mentioned? To "seal up" here means to put something away since it is no longer needed. Why would that which is

mentioned here no longer be needed **(2 Corinthians 1:20)**?

5. The last purpose mentioned may be rendered "to anoint a most holy place" or "to anoint a most holy person." What would be meant if "a most holy place" is the correct translation **(1 Kings 8:6, 10–13; 1 Corinthians 3:16)**? What would be the meaning if "a most holy person" is correct **(Luke 4:14–19)**? Why is there little ultimate difference between the two possible meanings **(John 2:19–22; Revelation 21:3, 22)**?

The "Sevens" of Blessing

Read **Daniel 9:25** in the translation above.

1. What event is designated by the expression "the going forth of a command to return and to rebuild Jerusalem" **(Isaiah 44:28; 45:1, 13; Ezra 1:1–4)**?

2. Ultimately from whom did this word go forth **(Daniel 9:23; Ezra 6:14)**?

3. This verse speaks of the coming of "an anointed one, a prince." For what Old Testament offices were men anointed **(Exodus 40:12–15; 1 Samuel 16:1, 12–13; 1 Kings 19:16)**? Therefore, who is designated by this phrase, "an anointed one, a prince," because He holds all of these offices **(Luke 1:32–33; 4:14–19; Hebrews 4:14)**?

According to the translation given above and the RSV, the anointed one will come after seven "sevens." The NIV translates this part of the verse as follows: "From the issuing of the decree to restore and rebuild Jerusalem until the Anointed One, the ruler, comes, there will be seven 'sevens,' and sixty-two 'sevens.' "

This difference in translation marks the first major difference between the traditional and typical messianic interpretations. The Masoretic (9th century A.D.) punctuation of the Hebrew text supports the rendering of the author and the RSV. Moreover, the translation of the New International Version presupposes a very unusual method of counting 69 weeks (see also the beginning of **Daniel 9:26**). These factors make interpretation D more likely to be correct, at least at this point in the passage.

4. To what does the rebuilding of Jerusalem in the latter part of **9:25** refer according to interpretation C **(Nehemiah 6:1)**? To what does it refer according to interpretation D **(Galatians 4:26)**? It is said that the city will be rebuilt "with plaza and moat." What would this mean according to interpretation C? according to interpretation D **(Matthew 16:18)**?

5. During what kind of times will this rebuilding take place? To what would this refer according to interpretation C **(Nehemiah 6:2)**? according to interpretation D **(Acts 14:22)**?

The End of the 69th "Seven"

Read **Daniel 9:26** in the translation given above.

1. This verse states that at the end of the 69th "seven" the anointed one "will be cut off and have no more." To what does this refer according to interpretation C **(Isaiah 53:8)**? According to interpretation D **(Matthew 24:21–24)**?

2. This verse also speaks of the coming of a second "prince." To whom does this refer according to interpretation C **(Matthew 24:1–2)?** according to interpretation D **(1 John 2:18)?**

3. **Daniel 9:26** says that there will be war until the end and that desolations are determined. With what statements of Jesus is this in harmony **(Matthew 24:3, 6–8)?**

4. According to this verse how will this second prince meet his end? To what important Old Testament event is this similar **(Exodus 14:26–28)?** What does this say about the end of this second prince? Would this portion of the verse fit in more readily with interpretation C or interpretation D?

The 70th "Seven"

Read **Daniel 9:27** in the translation given above.

The "seven" referred to in this verse refers to the 70th "seven."

Note what this verse says about a covenant. If interpretation C is correct, this refers to Christ fulfilling the old covenant of God with His people and establishing a new covenant for His church **(1 Corinthians 11:25).**

If interpretation D is correct, this predicts that Antichrist will try to win followers by seeming to offer the same good things Jesus really does give to His people.

1. What does this verse foretell about "sacrifice and offering," that is, about the worship carried on in the temple in Jerusalem? What would be meant here according to interpretation C **(Hebrews 10:11–18)?** According to interpretation D **(Revelation 13:4, 7–8)?**

Note that **Daniel 9:27** says that the one who makes desolate comes "on the wing of abominations." According to interpretation C this refers to the sacrifices and the like that continued in the Jerusalem temple after its fulfillment by Christ. This does not seem likely in view of the fact that many of the early believers (including Paul and Peter) continued to worship in the temple. According to interpretation D the abominations mentioned here are those committed by people during the heyday of Antichrist just prior to the end of time.

2. What will happen to "the one who makes desolate"? If interpretation D is correct, to what would this refer (**2 Thessalonians 2:8; Acts 17:31**)?

Further Considerations

1. There is nothing in this passage that gives us any information about what will mark the end of the 70 "sevens." In light of **Matthew 24:42** what does this tell us?

2. Assuming for the moment that interpretation D is the correct one, how many similarities can you find between what is said about Antichrist in **9:26–27** and what is said about Antiochus Epiphanes (a type of Antichrist) in **Daniel 8:11** and **25**?

The Word for Us

1. Who is at the center of the entire vision of **Daniel 9:24–27?** What is significant about that?

2. How does this passage illustrate the importance of the principle that we must let Scripture interpret Scripture?

3. What encouragement for faith is there for God's people in Daniel's vision of the 70 "sevens"?

Closing

Sing or read together "Lord, Keep Us Steadfast in Your Word":

Lord, keep us steadfast in Your Word;
Curb those who by deceit or sword
Would wrest the kingdom from Your Son
And bring to nought all He has done.

Lord Jesus Christ, Your pow'r make known,
For You are Lord of lords alone;
Defend Your holy Church that we
May sing Your praise triumphantly.

O Comforter of priceless worth,
Send peace and unity on earth;
Support us in our final strife
And lead us out of death to life.

Lesson 12

Daniel's Final Vision
(Part 1)

Theme Verse

"Now I have come to explain to you what will happen to your people in the future, for the vision concerns a time yet to come." **(Daniel 10:14)**

Goal

The goal of this lesson is that we may marvel at our God's control of the events of history and see in it His care and concern for us His people.

What's Going On Here?

The last three chapters of the book of Daniel consist of the prophet's record of a single vision he experienced very late in his lifetime. Because the vision is too lengthy to be adequately studied in one session, the final two lessons of this course are devoted to it.

This vision, especially as it is recorded in **chapter 11,** is one of the most unusual in all of Scripture. Whereas most of the predictions of the Bible contain a certain amount of indefiniteness and are rather general in character, **Daniel 11** gives a strikingly detailed and exact forecast of events that took place from the time of the Persian conquest of Babylon until about 165 B.C. This unusual feature has been the chief cause of the wide variety of interpretations given to the chapter.

As was the case with **chapter 9,** the various interpretations of the final vision of Daniel may be classified under three general headings. These three different interpretive approaches correspond to the four approaches we examined in the last lesson (the proponents of interpretations C and D are even more united in their understanding of this chapter than they were in their interpretation of **Daniel 9**). These three approaches are as follows:

(A) The "critical" or "liberal" interpretation of the book of Daniel seizes on **chapter 11** as the ultimate proof of the correctness of its approach. **Daniel 11** is very detailed and accurate in its description of historical events from the time of the Persians until 165. However, from that point onward the prophecy of this chapter becomes much more general and indefinite, like many of the other prophecies of the Old Testament. Critics cite this as proof that the author of Daniel was really an individual living in 165 B.C. who wished to give his fellow Jews encouragement in the face of their persecutions under Antiochus Epiphanes, ruler of Syria. This unknown author wrote his book under the guise of prophecy, claiming to be a famous character from Israel's past who had predicted the history of the Near East from the time of the Persians until 165 with incredible detail and accuracy. However, when the real author attempted to actually predict the future, he was forced to lapse into very unspecific language, and this change from the detailed to the indefinite can be easily detected in **Daniel 11:40.**

This entire approach rests on the assumption that it is impossible for **Daniel 11** to foretell the future in such detail. For anyone who accepts the Scriptures as actually being the Word of God, this approach must be rejected.

(B) The dispensationalist or premillennial interpreters of Daniel attempt to read **chapter 11** as a blueprint of history leading right up to the end of the world. As was the case with **chapter 9,** these interpreters attempt to use this chapter to forecast the exact time of the end of the world. The same warnings and criticisms voiced in the last lesson about this method of interpreting the Scriptures also apply here.

(C) The third approach to interpreting this chapter is at least as old as the time of the church father Jerome, who died in the year A.D. 420. Advocates of this method of interpretation agree with the proponents of method A that **Daniel 11** offers a detailed description of events from 538 to 165 B.C., but they disagree with the proponents of method A in seeing this chapter as being written not after the fact but by the biblical character Daniel in advance of any of these occurrences. The change from specific to general language (which really begins more in **verse 36** than in **verse 40**) is due not to the real author's inability to predict what is yet to come; rather, it is to be explained by the change in subject matter. The afflictions of God's people under Antiochus Epiphanes are types or foreshadowings of the hardships the people of God face throughout their lives in this fallen and hostile world, especially just prior to the second coming of Christ. Beginning with **verse 36,** Daniel moves away from detailed predictions of historical facts to predictions of the difficulties God's people will face at any and every time in history. Thus, the latter verses of **Daniel 11** describe the ultimate meaning of history for believers. This last method of interpretation is, of course, the one that will be followed in this study.

Searching the Scriptures

Introduction to the Vision

Read **Daniel 10:1–3.**

1. What would be the significance of dating the vision within the reign of Cyrus, both in terms of Daniel's age and with reference to the role of Cyrus in the history of God's people **(Ezra 1:1–4)?**

2. Why might Daniel have been mourning and fasting **(Ezra 4:4–5)?** What else did he do as an expression of his sorrow **(2 Samuel 14:2)?**

3. What things are told us in **verse 1** about the revelation to Daniel on this occasion?

The Heavenly Messenger

Read **Daniel 10:4–9.**

1. What did the appearance of the heavenly messenger **(10:5–6)** suggest about his identity? In spite of this, what items of information about him indicate that this was not an appearance of God Himself **(10:11, 13)?**

2. Compare the reaction of Daniel's companions **(10:7)** to that of those who were accompanying Saul when he was met by our Lord on the road to

Damascus **(Acts 26:12–14; 9:3–7)**. What is the significance of these reactions?

3. What was the meaning of Daniel's reaction to the appearance of the heavenly messenger **(10:8–9)**?

Preparation for the Vision

Read **Daniel 10:10–11:1.**

1. How did the angel's words and actions in **10:11–12** reassure Daniel?

2. What had this angel and Michael done on behalf of the people of God **(10:13)**? Read **10:21** and also **Revelation 12:7–10.** Who is Michael, and what is the meaning of his and the other angels contending against others on behalf of the people of God? What insight does this give us into the identity of the "prince" of the kingdom of Persia?

In **Daniel 10** the "prince of Persia" was persuading the Persian rulers against the people of Judah in their efforts to rebuild the temple of God in Jerusalem. Since the fallen angels (devils) work on behalf of the evil peoples and kingdoms of the world, it is necessary for the good angels, over whom is the archangel Michael, to do battle with these. In **Revelation 12** the war in heaven between Michael and the angels against the devil and his angels indicates that such battles are ongoing, although the victory for Michael is assured because of the death and resurrection of Christ.

The angel who was speaking with Daniel had remained among the kings of Persia to influence them for good, so that eventually they would allow the people of God to finish rebuilding the temple and the city (as recounted in the books of Ezra, Nehemiah, Haggai, and Zechariah). This makes it even more likely that Daniel was fasting and mourning on account of the opposition faced by those attempting to rebuild the temple. In answer to Daniel's prayers the angel not only assured him that he had been working for good for God's people in the court of the Persian king but also gave him the vision that followed, revealing God's care over His people in their Promised Land, which would continue in spite of the many persecutions and afflictions they would yet face. The vision assured Daniel (and us his readers) that the victory belongs to God's people.

3. What evidence is there in the angel's words to Daniel that the vision he would reveal also had something to do with the New Testament era? Compare **10:14** with **Hebrews 1:2; Acts 2:17;** and **2 Timothy 3:1**. (A literal translation of **10:14** would read in part, "what will happen to your people in the latter days.")

4. What continued signs of unworthiness on Daniel's part are recounted in **10:15–17,** and how did the angel again strengthen him **(10:16, 18–19)?**

5. Whom would the angel overcome, and who was yet to come forth **(10:20)?** What empire does **Daniel 11:1** imply had also been defeated by Michael and the angel who spoke to Daniel?

The Vision Itself

As was mentioned previously, **Daniel 11** is somewhat unique among biblical prophecies in that it gives a detailed description of future historical events. Nevertheless, it must be stressed that some occurrences that might have been mentioned have been passed by without comment. Therefore, we must not expect the chapter to recount every individual who might have played some role in the history of the Holy Land of that time.

Persia and Greece

Read **Daniel 11:2–4.**

1. How many more Persian kings were mentioned, and what would the last of these attempt to do **(11:2)**?

2. What is said of "a mighty king," and what would be the fate of his empire **(11:3–4)**?

Egypt and Syria

Read **Daniel 11:5–20** verse by verse as you work through the following section.

Note the two principal characters mentioned in **11:5.** The king of the south was Ptolemy I, one of the chief generals of Alexander and the first king of the Egyptian portion of Alexander's empire. One of his commanders was Seleucus I, who was also one of Alexander's generals, but who for a time served under Ptolemy. Eventually Seleucus came to control an empire of his own, which included Syria. The empires established by these two men waged war on and off, with first Egypt then later Syria having control over the land of Palestine. The following chart may help in sorting out the various kings mentioned in these verses. (The dates for these rulers and the relationships between them are given on the chart on page 1320 of the Concordia Self-Study Bible.)

Daniel 11	Egypt	Syria
5	Ptolemy I	Seleucus I
no mention		Antiochus I
6	Ptolemy II	Antiochus II
7–9	Ptolemy III	Seleucus II
10–13	Ptolemy IV	Seleucus III/
		Antiochus III
14	Ptolemy IV/	
	Ptolemy V	
15–19	Ptolemy V	Antiochus III
20		Seleucus IV
21–35		Antiochus IV (Epiphanes)

1. Does it appear from **11:6** that the alliance mentioned there would be a successful one?

2. Who would have the advantage in the conflict described in **11:7–9**?

3. What would the sons of the king of the north do **(11:10)**? Who would gain the first advantage in the ongoing battle of Egypt and Syria **(11:11–12)**? How would the fortunes later be reversed **(11:13)**?

4. What difficulty would the king of Egypt then experience, and how would some of the people of Judea ("your own people") react to this development **(11:14)**? How would the king of Syria take advantage of this **(11:15–16)**?

5. What would the king of Syria attempt next, and would it be successful **(11:17)**? What would happen to this king on a subsequent campaign **(11:18)**, and what would he be forced to do as a result **(11:19)**?

6. What would the successor of this last king attempt **(11:20)**? Would his attempt be successful?

A Glimpse Ahead

Next time we will complete our study of Daniel's final vision. We will see how the events here foretold have application to the church of every age. We will also hear the good news of God's deliverance of His people in the face of all their hardship.

The Word for Us

1. Why are the biblical teachings about angels reassuring and comforting for us?

2. Why is it important to teach correctly about angels? How can teaching wrongly about angels be a false comfort or even harmful?

3. Consider the material of this lesson in light of **Matthew 10:29–31.** What encouragement for faith do we find in God's care for even the minute, seemingly insignificant details of life?

Closing

Sing or read together the following stanzas of "Stars of the Morning, So Gloriously Bright":

Stars of the morning, so gloriously bright,
Filled with celestial resplendence and light,
These, where no darkness the glory can dim,
Praise the Thrice Holy One, serving but Him.

These are Your ministers, these are Your own,
Lord God of Sabaoth, nearest Your throne;
These are Your messengers, these whom You send,
Helping Your helpless ones, Helper and Friend.

Still let them be with us, still let them fight,
Lord of angelic hosts, battling for right,
Till, where their anthems they ceaselessly pour,
We with the angels may bow and adore.

Lesson 13

Daniel's Final Vision (Part 2)

Theme Verse

"Multitudes who sleep in the dust of the earth will awake: some to everlasting life, others to shame and everlasting contempt. Those who are wise will shine like the brightness of the heavens, and those who lead many to righteousness, like the stars for ever and ever." **(Daniel 12:2–3)**

Goal

The goal of this lesson is that we may see in the final vision and throughout the book of Daniel God's word of encouragement for us that in spite of the severe afflictions that are certain to come our way, the victory is ours through faith in Christ Jesus.

What's Going On Here?

In the last lesson we began studying the final vision given to Daniel and saw how the Lord's angel gave him a detailed prediction of historical events that would affect God's people. In this lesson we will continue this study, seeing how the prophecy moves into a general description of the way things will always be for the people of God who are in this world and then concludes with a message of great hope and encouragement for all believers.

Searching the Scriptures

Antiochus Epiphanes

Read **Daniel 11:21–35** verse by verse as you work through the following section. The historical character who is described by way of prophecy in these verses is Antiochus IV, king of Syria from 175–164 B.C. He called himself "Epiphanes," which was virtually a claim to deity (as our Epiphany season celebrates Christ's revelation of His deity). The Jews, who smarted under his oppressive rule, which is outlined in these verses, called him "Epimanes," meaning "madman."

1. What does **11:21** tell us about the way in which Antiochus would gain dominion over the kingdom of Syria?

Verses 22–24 describe this king's exploits in battle. Antiochus had some successes in war **(v. 22)** through alliances and further intrigue **(v. 23)**. The reference to a "prince of the covenant" **(v. 22)** may refer to a Judean high priest who lost his life during the time of Antiochus. **Verse 24** describes his campaign in Egypt, after which he was able "only for a time" to gain some advantage by currying the favor of others through giving them some of his spoils of war.

Read **11:25–26** which foretold another campaign by Antiochus against Egypt. The victory by Antiochus was due largely to the fact that the king of Egypt (Ptolemy VI) was let down by even his closest supporters.

2. What does **11:27** tell us about further relationships between these two kings? Why would their evil efforts prove to be a failure for both of them?

Read **11:28**. After this expedition to Egypt Antiochus returned to his homeland in 169 but only after massacring 40,000 Jews, enslaving many others, and plundering valuables from the temple.

3. Who would foil the efforts of Antiochus when he would attempt yet another expedition against Egypt **(11:29–30)?** As a result against whom would he direct his anger? To whom, therefore, would he give preferential treatment?

4. What three things does **11:31** mention that Antiochus would do? How do the words of Jesus in **Matthew 24:15–24** indicate that the persecutions under Antiochus were typical of the hardships that the people of God will face throughout history?

Read **Daniel 11:32–35.** Some Jews were enticed to follow the program of Antiochus. Others remained faithful to their God, as Daniel had often done while in Babylon. For a time (about three years) those who remained faithful were subject to torture and martyrdom. Their heroic fidelity to the true God is recounted in the apocryphal books of **1 and 2 Maccabees.**

From Antiochus to Antichrist

Read **Daniel 11:36–39. Verse 36** marks a transition point in Daniel's final vision. A great deal of attention is devoted to Antiochus Epiphanes in this vision, because he and his opposition toward God's people serve as a type of Antichrist. The name "Antichrist" refers to a principle at work throughout the New Testament era. Antichrist claims to impart religious truth, while its teaching actually opposes true faith.

Beginning with **11:36,** the description of Antiochus, a type of Antichrist, fades into the background and eventually disappears altogether, being replaced with a description of Antichrist itself. For this reason the interpretation of **Daniel 11:36** and following is quite difficult. But a comparison of this passage with **2 Thessalonians 2,** the most detailed description of Antichrist in all of Scripture (in which Antichrist is referred to as "the man of lawlessness" and "the man doomed to destruction" **[v. 3]**), helps us to see that Antichrist and not Antiochus Epiphanes himself is the subject of these verses.

1. According to **11:36–37** against whom does this figure set himself? Compare this with Paul's description of Antichrist in **2 Thessalonians 2:4.** How long will he have success **(Daniel 11:36)?** What indication is there in this verse that all of this is permitted by God?

Note the attitude Antichrist will take toward the faith of Daniel's predecessors in the faith (11:37–38). Daniel 11:37 seems to say that Antichrist comes from within the outward association of the people of God, although he rejects the God of his predecessors.

2. What does Antichrist do for those who align themselves with him (11:39)?

The Defeat of Antichrist

Read Daniel 11:40–45.

1. Note the indication of time given in 11:40. How does this help to designate Antichrist as the subject of these verses (compare 2 Thessalonians 2:1–3)? What are the circumstances in which Antichrist will find himself (Daniel 11:40)?

2. Who is attacked by Antichrist and who is aligned with him (11:41)? Why can we understand these latter ones as symbols for all the enemies of God and His people (1 Samuel 14:47)?

In 11:42 Egypt, another ancient nemesis of the people of God, probably stands for the fallen world in so far as it is allied with Antichrist. As we can see from 11:43, initially Antichrist does have success, just as did those hindering the rebuilding of the temple at the time when Daniel received this vision. Yet eventually God's people triumphed in rebuilding the temple. In time God's people will triumph when Antichrist is defeated.

3. What is the last object of his hostilities (11:45)? Why will he not be able to escape from his future destruction (11:45; see also 2 Thessalonians 2:8)?

The Deliverance of the People of God

Read **Daniel 12:1–3.** The distress of the times just prior to the end will be the most severe of all. The angel Michael is again presented as the guardian angel of the people of Israel, that is, of the people of God. Here and in **Revelation 12** he is designated as one through whom God delivers His people from the assaults of evil. The book mentioned in **Daniel 12:1** is the Book of Life (see **Revelation 20:15**), a heavenly register of those whom God has chosen from eternity to be saved.

Who are those "who sleep in the dust of the earth" **(Daniel 12:2; Genesis 3:19)**, and what will happen to them **(John 5:24–29)?**

The wise **(Daniel 12:3)** are those who have true wisdom **(Proverbs 9:10)**, that is, a saving relationship with God through faith in Jesus Christ. Those who know Christ seek to lead others to Him that they too might be clothed with His righteousness. In the words of **Daniel 12:3,** they "lead many to righteousness." Shining like the brightness of the heavens and the stars is a description of the wonderful glory of eternal life.

Read **Daniel 12:4.** The sealing of the book (perhaps a reference to the entire book of Daniel) is a command to preserve it for future generations. The book was to be sealed until the end of time, for its visions and prophecies take us to the very end of the age. These revelations of God's will and plan have been given to succeeding generations in order that they may have knowledge of God's care for and protection of His people.

The Conclusion of the Prophecy

Read **Daniel 12:5–13.** The questioner in **12:6** asks how long it will be until these things are completed, that is, how long it will be until the end. It is interesting to note that the Hebrew word used for "river" in these verses is most often used in the Old Testament for the Nile River of Egypt. Here it refers to the Tigris **(10:4)**. Perhaps this is a subtle indication that the salvation here foretold is a new exodus.

1. What did the angel do to indicate the solemnity of his answer **(12:7)?** Compare the angel's answer with **7:25.** What will accompany the completion of all these things?

When the prophet indicated that he still did not understand the meaning of all of this, he was informed that they pertain to the time of the end. Therefore, he was not to inquire into them further but was to faithfully go about his business ("Go your way, Daniel" [12:9]), since these things would only be able to be understood in the life to come. More than one interpreter of Scripture has expressed the longing that all students of the visions of Daniel should take these words to heart and cease from trying to decipher from these visions a timetable for the end of the world.

2. How does 12:10 summarize the message of the final vision and indeed of the entire book of Daniel?

Both figures given in 12:11–12 add up to a little more than three and a half years or a little more than half of seven, the number of completeness. This is another indication that the time of trial and persecution here described will be shortened as God comes for the deliverance of His people. Therefore, a blessing is pronounced on those who remain faithful until the end (12:12). It may be noted that neither of these designations of time fit into the history of Antiochus Epiphanes (the attempted "liberal" and "critical" interpretation) nor into any timetable for the end of the world (as proposed by dispensationalist interpreters).

3. Note the instruction given to the prophet in the concluding verse of his book. What fate would befall him (and will befall all of us)? What message of encouragement for faith did the angel give him? Why is this message of encouragement ours as well (1 Corinthians 15:20–23)?

The Word for Us

1. What new insights into or appreciation for the apocalyptic writings of the Bible have you gained from this course of study?

2. What are the most important lessons of comfort and encouragement you have learned from your study of Daniel?

Closing

Sing or read together the following stanza from "Jesus Lives! The Victory's Won":

Jesus lives! The vict'ry's won!
Death no longer can appall me;
Jesus lives! Death's reign is done!
From the grave will Christ recall me.
Brighter scenes will then commence;
This shall be my confidence.

DANIEL
Encouragement for Faith

Leaders Notes

Preparing to Teach Daniel

The book of Daniel includes some of the most challenging items for study in all of God's Word. The materials in these notes are designed to help you in leading others through this portion of the Holy Scriptures. Nevertheless, this booklet is to be an aid to and not a substitute for your own study of and preparation for teaching the book of Daniel.

If you have the opportunity, you will find it helpful to make use of other biblical reference works in the course of your study. The two best commentaries on the book of Daniel are those written by Herbert C. Leupold (*Exposition of Daniel*, 1949, reprinted 1969 by Baker, Grand Rapids) and Edward J. Young (*The Prophecy of Daniel: A Commentary*, Grand Rapids: Eerdmans, 1949). Although it is not strictly a commentary, the section on Daniel in *The Word Becoming Flesh* by Horace Hummel (St. Louis: Concordia, 1979) also contains much that is of value for the proper interpretation of this biblical book.

Group Bible Study

Group Bible study means mutual learning from one another under the guidance of a leader. The Bible is an inexhaustible resource. No one person can discover all it has to offer. In a class many eyes see many things and can apply them to many life situations. The leader should resist the temptation to "give the answers" and so act as an "authority." This teaching approach stifles participation by individual members and can actually hamper learning. As a general rule the teacher is not to "give interpretation" but to "develop interpreters." Of course there are times when the leader should and must share insights and information gained by his or her own deeper research. The ideal class is one in which the leader guides class members through the lesson and engages them in meaningful sharing and discussion at all points, leading them to a summary of the lesson at the close. As a general rule, don't explain what the learners can discover by themselves.

Have a chalkboard and chalk or newsprint and marker available to emphasize significant points of the lesson. Rephrase your inquiries or the inquiries of participants as questions, problems, or issues. This provokes thought. Keep discussion to the point. List on the chalkboard or newsprint the answers given. Then determine the most vital points made in the discussion. Ask additional questions to fill gaps.

The aim of every Bible study is to help people grow spiritually, not merely in biblical and theological knowledge, but in Christian thinking and living. This means growth in Christian attitudes, insights, and skills for Christian living. The focus of this course must be the church and the world of our day. The guiding question will be this: What does the Lord teach us for life today through the book of Daniel.

Pace Your Teaching

The lessons in this course of study are designed for a study session of at least an hour in length. If it is the desire and intent of the class to complete an entire lesson each session, it will be necessary for you to keep careful watch over the class time. At times it may be necessary for you to summarize the content of certain answers or biblical references in order to preserve time. Asking various class members to look up different Bible passages and to read them aloud to the rest of the class will save time over having every class member look up each reference.

Also, you may not want to cover every question in each lesson. This may lead to undue haste and frustration. Be selective. Pace your teaching. Spend no more than 5–10 minutes with "Theme Verse," "Goal," and "What's Going On Here?" Take time to go into the text by topic, but not word by word. Get the sweep of meaning. Occasionally stop to help the class gain understanding of a word or concept. Allow approximately 10–15 minutes for "The Word for Us." Allowing approximately 5 minutes for "Closing" and announcements, you will notice, allows you only approximately 30 minutes for "Searching the Scriptures."

Should your group have more than a one-hour class period, you can take it more leisurely. But do not allow any lesson to drag and become tiresome. Keep it moving. Keep it alive. Keep it meaningful. Eliminate some questions and restrict yourself to those questions most meaningful to the members of the class. If most members study the text at home, they can report their findings, and the time gained can be applied to relating the lesson to life.

Good Preparation

Good preparation by the leader usually affects the pleasure and satisfaction the class will experience.

Suggestions to the Leader for Using the Study Guide

The Lesson Pattern

This set of 13 lessons is based on a timely Old Testament book—Daniel. The material is designed to aid *Bible study*, that is, to aid a consideration of the written Word of God, with discussion and personal application growing out of the text at hand.

The typical lesson is divided into these sections:
1. Theme Verse
2. Goal

3. What's Going On Here?
4. Searching the Scriptures
5. The Word for Us
6. Closing

"Theme Verse," "Goal," and "What's Going On Here?" give the leader assistance in arousing the interest of the group in the concepts of the lesson. Here the leader stimulates minds. Do not linger too long over the introductory remarks.

"Searching the Scriptures" provides the real spadework necessary for Bible study. Here the class digs, uncovers, and discovers; it gets the facts and observes them. Comments from the leader are needed only to the extent that they help the group understand the text. The same is true of looking up the indicated parallel passages. The questions in this guide, arranged under subheadings and corresponding to sections within the text, are intended to help the participants discover the meaning of the text.

Having determined what the text says, the class is ready to apply the message. Having heard, read, marked, and learned the Word of God, proceed to digest it inwardly through discussion, evaluation, and application. This is done, as this guide suggests, by taking the truths found in Daniel and applying them to the world and Christianity, in general, and then to personal Christian life. Class time may not permit discussion of all questions and topics. In preparation the leader may need to select one or two and focus on them. These questions bring God's message to the individual Christian. Close the session by reviewing one important truth from the lesson.

Remember, the Word of God is sacred, but this study guide is not. The notes in this section offer only guidelines and suggestions. Do not hesitate to alter the guidelines or substitute others to meet your needs and the needs of the participants. Adapt your teaching plan to your class and your class period. Good teaching directs the learner to discover for himself or herself. For the teacher this means directing the learner, not giving the learner answers. Choose the verses that should be looked up in Scripture. What discussion questions will you ask? At what points? Write them in the margin of your study guide. Involve class members, but give them clear directions. What practical actions might you propose for the week following the lesson? Which of the items do you consider most important for your class?

How will you best use your teaching period? Do you have 45 minutes? an hour? or an hour and a half? If time is short, what should you cut? Learn to become a wise steward of class time.

Be sure to take time to summarize the lesson, or have a class member do it. Plan brief opening and closing devotions, using members of the class.

Remember to pray frequently for yourself and your class. May God the Holy Spirit bless your study and your leading of others into the comforting truths of God's Christ-centered Word.

Lesson 1
Introduction and Overview

The Class Session
Have volunteers read "Theme Verses," "Goal," and "What's Going On Here?"

Searching the Scriptures
Characteristics of Apocalyptic Literature
Read aloud or ask a volunteer to read the introductory material in this section. In connection with points 1 and 2, point out that for Christians the victory is already assured because of Christ's resurrection. This victory will be completed when our Lord comes again on the Last Day to raise us from the dead so that we may live with Him forever in heaven. In connection with point 5, note that a knowledge of the religious, historical, and cultural background of an apocalyptic writing helps us understand the symbolism it uses. Much of the symbolism of the book of Daniel may be understood in light of the historical circumstances affecting the people of Israel at the time when Daniel was written. (The historical background of the book of Daniel is covered later in this lesson.) By understanding the symbols used in an apocalyptic writing such as Daniel, one is greatly aided in uncovering its proper (literal) interpretation.

Quickly lead the class through an examination of the passages listed in the study guide in order that all may get a feel for Daniel as an example of apocalyptic literature. Or you might want to divide the verses among class members and have them read the passages aloud and note which characteristic(s) of apocalyptic are evident.

The Interpretation of Apocalyptic Literature
The following information may be used to supplement the readings from the study guide.

1. This is the usual approach of those who employ the historical-critical method of biblical interpretation.

2. This method is often employed by those who advocate a dispensationalist interpretation (including "the rapture" and a literal millennium) of the apocalyptic portions of the Bible. In this course, we will have occasion to take issue with such interpretations of the book of Daniel.

Author
That an individual named Daniel who lived during Israel's exile in Baby-

lon could have been the author of this particular book of the Bible is universally denied by those who employ the historical-critical method of biblical interpretation. This denial of danielic authorship stems from a further denial of the ability of the author of the book to have actually predicted the events described therein (particularly in the latter chapters of the book). It is, therefore, necessary to emphasize that a failure to attribute this work to the historical Daniel amounts to an attack on (1) the reliability of the Scriptures; (2) the authority of the Lord Jesus Himself (for it is He who ascribes the book to Daniel in the words recorded in **Matthew 24:15**); and (3) the predictive nature of Old Testament prophecy. Thus, the question of the authorship of this book is an important one.

Historical Circumstances

1–5. The identity of the four world empires of Daniel will be examined in greater detail in other lessons. They are Babylonia, Medo-Persia, Greece, and Rome. The purpose of this portion of the lesson is simply to acquaint the class with the historical situation of the book of Daniel. The following paragraphs may serve as a useful supplement to the material in the study guide.

During the last quarter of the seventh century B.C., the Assyrian Empire was conquered by the Babylonians and the Medes. In 605 Nebuchadnezzar, who was leading the Babylonian army for his ailing father, won a decisive victory over the Egyptians who were attempting to stop Babylon from becoming the dominant power. Later that year Nebuchadnezzar's father died, and Nebuchadnezzar became the king of Babylon. Nebuchadnezzar made several excursions into Palestine, each time taking some of the people of Judah into exile and finally destroying Judah and Jerusalem in 586.

In 539 Babylon fell to Cyrus, king of the Medes and Persians. It was Cyrus who allowed the people of Judah to return to their homeland, so that by 516 they had rebuilt the Jerusalem temple. In the years following 334 the empire of the Medes and Persians gradually fell to Alexander the Great of Greece. After Alexander's death in 323, there was a protracted struggle for control of his empire.

Two of his generals, Ptolemy (who came to control Egypt) and Seleucus (who came to control Syria) became the heads of dynasties that alternated in gaining control over Palestine. Beginning in 175 a descendant of Seleucus named Antiochus IV Epiphanes ruled Palestine. In 167 he attempted to institute the worship of Greek gods in Palestine, including in the temple itself. The Jews rebelled, first under the leadership of Mattathias Hasmoneas and then under the leadership of his son Judas Maccabaeus. In 164 the Jews regained control of the temple. Their act of rededicating the temple is the origin of the festival of Hanukkah.

The Maccabean revolt continued off and on until 142 when the Jews won complete political independence. They enjoyed self-rule until 63 when the Roman general Pompey gained control of Palestine for Rome. The Romans still ruled the Holy Land when the events recorded in the New Testament took place.

Outline and Language

Have a member of the class read these two sections.

The Word for Us

1–2. Class members may share responses. The Scriptures indicate that in this life the unbelieving will take advantage of and even persecute God's people. Thus, until Christ's return we will always find ourselves in circumstances at least somewhat similar to those of the time of the book of Daniel.

3. Among ideas that may be shared are understanding the symbolism of the book, knowing the historical circumstances, reading the book in light of all of Scripture, and seeing the relationship of the book's message to Jesus Christ.

Closing

Follow the suggestion in the study guide.

Lesson 2

The Testing of the Four Young Men

The Class Session

Have volunteers read "Theme Verses," "Goal," and "What's Going On Here?"

Searching the Scriptures

The Historical Setting

The following information is included for those who are interested in the dating systems used in the ancient Near East and how differing dates can be reconciled. Don't spend a lot of class time on this issue. Interested students can read this information outside of class time.

Different calendars were employed in the ancient Near East. In one ancient calendar, the new year began in the fall of the year; in another calendar, the beginning of the new year took place in the spring. This difference of approximately one-half year would mean that an event designated as having taken place within a given year in one calendar might be counted in the previous or following year in the other calendar. Compare for example **Daniel 1:1** with **Jeremiah 25:1.** If Daniel and Jeremiah are using differing calendars to reckon time, this could easily account for Daniel dating these events of the first year of Nebuchadnezzar's reign in the third year of the rule of Jehoiakim, while according to the calendar used by Jeremiah it was already the fourth year of Jehoiakim's reign when Nebuchadnezzar became king of Babylon. This use of different calendars could also account for the one-year difference in dating the various deportations of Judah's citizens to Babylon as reported in Jeremiah and the book of Kings.

Another factor that needs to be considered and that could explain the one year difference between these various accounts is the use in the ancient world of different methods of reckoning the years of a king's rule. In "method A" the first partial year of a king's reign was counted as year 1, the year that began with the New Year's Day following the king's coming to power being counted as year 2. In "method B" the first partial year of a king's rule was considered his "accession year," and the year that began with the New Year's Day following the king's coming to power was counted as year 1.

In attempting to translate these biblical datings into the modern designation of years before Christ, one must also keep in mind that in neither of the ancient calendars referred to above does the beginning of the new year take place at the same time as it does in the modern Gregorian calendar. Therefore, there is some overlapping between the years of a king's reign and modern-year designations. This overlapping means that there may be some uncertainty as to when an ancient event is to be dated in our modern system of dating.

Those desiring more information are invited to consult the commentaries of Young and Leupold referred to in "Preparing to Teach Daniel" at the beginning of the leaders notes, as well as Edwin R. Thiele's book *The Mysterious Numbers of the Hebrew Kings*, pp. 155–73.

1. Apparently Jehoiakim surrendered to the vastly superior forces of Nebuchadnezzar without a fight. The subjection of Judah by Babylon gave those with a pagan worldview the idea that the gods of Babylon were more powerful than the God of Judah. Nebuchadnezzar drove home his belief in the superiority of his gods by taking some of the articles from the temple

and putting them in the temple of his god in Babylon. However, Daniel makes it clear that the Lord delivered Judah into the hands of Nebuchadnezzar.

2. The Lord was punishing Judah for its idolatry, bloodshed, and injustice.

3. The vessels Nebuchadnezzar took from the Jerusalem temple were not returned until Babylon had fallen to Cyrus, who permitted them to be taken back to Jerusalem by the returning exiles. By that time the vessels had been in foreign hands for nearly 70 years.

Introduction of the Main Characters

1. The young Hebrews were of royal stock or nobles; some perhaps were descendants of Hezekiah. They were spoils of war and were to become courtiers for the king of Babylon.

2. Daniel and his companions later functioned as wise men. Moses, the great man of God, was trained in the wisdom of the Egyptians.

3. The giving of a new name in these instances implied the superiority of the one giving the name over those to whom the name was given. In the case of the four youths of **Daniel 1** this also probably implied a superiority of the gods of Babylon over the God of Judah.

In the case of the two kings of Judah, their names were changed to ones having almost the same meaning: Eliakim ("God sets up") to Jehoiakim ("the LORD sets up") and Mattaniah ("gift of the LORD") to Zedekiah ("the LORD is righteous" or "righteousness of the LORD").

The Fidelity of the Four Young Men

1. It is likely that portions of the meat and wine may have been offered as sacrifices to Babylonian gods and to eat and drink them would have amounted to joining in the worship of the king's gods. Also the meat may often have been unclean and not slaughtered in such a way as to drain the blood. There were also other regulations about food preparation given by God to His people that would not have been followed by those who prepared Nebuchadnezzar's food.

2. Daniel exhibited courage in resolving not to eat the food, respect for those in charge of him by asking to be excused from eating the food, and wisdom in suggesting an alternative.

3. The favor and power of the Lord enabled Daniel's plan to succeed. First the Lord gave Daniel favor with those in charge of him. Then the Lord supplied Daniel and his three friends with good health.

4. The four young men do not seek to rebel against Nebuchadnezzar. In fact, eventually they would serve in his government. As Jeremiah would later direct, they became good citizens of their new homeland.

The Progress of the Four Young Men

1. The Lord enabled Daniel and his friends to have success in their instruction and to prosper in it. Yet their wisdom was always subject to their faith in the Lord. Hence, they would not allow their learning or their new positions of prestige to lead them away from the Lord; neither the temptations of persecution nor those of prosperity enticed them away.

2. In addition to the blessings Daniel shared with his three friends, he was also blessed with the prophetic gift, which he used in service to the Lord, to whom he gave all the glory for his gift. In this respect his story is not unlike that of Joseph in Egypt.

3. At the end of the period of training, Daniel and his three friends were found to be superior to all the others. The king, therefore, picked them to "stand" before him, that is, to be of service to him in his government.

4. The superior abilities with which the Lord blessed this foursome eventually led to their appointment as high-ranking officials in the government of Nebuchadnezzar.

5. In 539 B.C. Babylon fell to Cyrus, king of the Medes and Persians. This Cyrus allowed the Judean exiles to return to their homeland. From **Daniel 1:21** and **10:1,** we see that Daniel was active for the remainder of the Babylonian supremacy, a period of nearly 70 years. The point of the time notation here is not only that faithful Daniel had a prominent place in Babylonian government throughout its duration but also that God's faithful believer would outlast the nation that at present was holding him as an exile. The God of Judah, not the gods of Babylon, was the one worth following.

The Word for Us

1. Empowered by the Lord, Daniel and his friends endured and remained faithful to God in faith-challenging circumstances. And the Lord enabled them to prosper in the midst of these difficult circumstances. In their particular circumstances in life, believers may be called on to suffer for Christ's sake. But the Lord will remain faithful to them and empower them to follow Him even unto death. Since they died with Him (when He died on the cross **[Galatians 2:20]**), they will also live with Him. If they endure in the one true faith, they will also reign with Him.

2. A general principle to guide our decision-making in this area is that the Christian must obey God rather than people when the latter command what God has forbidden or forbid what God has commanded. Like Daniel, Christians can use tact and wisdom in attempting to deal with the situation, while at the same time not bowing to pressure to disobey the Lord. And they can seek the Lord's guidance and intervention in prayer.

3. Answers will vary. One possible answer to this question concerns the way Baptism is administered. Complete immersion is a valid method of Baptism. However, since certain denominations have long insisted that it is the only valid method, Lutherans have generally used another method. The whole issue of the things God has neither commanded nor forbidden could be the focus of a separate study. **1 Corinthians 8** and **Romans 14** are principal biblical references; see also article 10 of the Formula of Concord.

Closing

Follow the suggestion in the study guide.

Lesson 3

The Fall of World Empires

The Class Session

Have volunteers read "Theme Verse," "Goal," and "What's Going On Here?"

Searching the Scriptures

Nebuchadnezzar's Dream

Briefly remind the class that **Daniel 2:4b–7:28** was written in Aramaic and comprises the largest Aramaic portion of the Old Testament.

It could have been that Nebuchadnezzar could not remember the dream. But in light of **verse 9** he may not have forgotten it but was instead testing his wise men to see if they could prove the truth of their interpretation by also revealing the content of the dream. The cruelty and arrogance of ancient monarchs is well known, so that Nebuchadnezzar's harsh demand is in keeping with what we otherwise know of his (and other ancient despots') character. Turning a condemned man's home into a rubbish dump or even a public latrine was a not uncommon practice in the ancient Near East for adding insult and disgrace to injury.

The Dilemma of the Wise Men

1. The wise men of Nebuchadnezzar sensed that the king was in a foul mood. They hoped by their carefully chosen words to "buy some time" (as

the Aramaic idiom in **verse 8** has it) until the king relented from his unreasonable demand.

2. The term *Babylon* may here refer only to the capital city of the empire (contrast the wording of **2:48–3:1**), so that only the wise men there were to be put to death. **Verse 13** seems to suppose a general roundup of these wise men for a public execution. This would give Daniel a little time for the meetings with Arioch and the king that are described in the following verses.

3. Daniel displayed the wisdom and trust in God that were described in **chapter 1.**

The Revelation

1. That the God of Judah should be called "the God of the heavens" (in literal translation) is significant for two reasons: (1) The dream that is the subject of this chapter tells of how the various kingdoms of the earth will all fall before the everlasting God of Judah. (2) The religion of Babylon, which the subjugation of Judah had supposedly proven to be superior to the faith of God's people, was concerned a great deal with the heavenly bodies. In contrast to this, the point is made that the God of Judah is the God (i.e., Creator) of the heavens.

2. In this time of trouble Daniel sought out the support of fellow believers. Christians are encouraged by the Scriptures to do as Daniel did in this situation.

3. *Mystery* and *revelation* are important terms not only in this chapter but also in the writings of the Dead Sea community. This sect regarded the time of the Old Testament to be a mystery that was revealed by the teachings of their leader, the Teacher of Righteousness. In a somewhat similar way Paul speaks of the Old Testament as a mystery that has now been revealed in New Testament times to be Christ as Savior also for the Gentiles. This revelation is communicated to us by the apostolic witness of the Scriptures and is proclaimed through the sharing of the Gospel.

4. Daniel's initial response was not to run to the king with the answer to his demand but to offer a prayer of praise and thanksgiving to God. God must give wisdom, which the Babylonian wise men could only pretend to have, and so Daniel thanks Him for wisdom. The God of Daniel is the one who sets up and deposes kings, and He revealed to Daniel that He would establish and remove four separate kingdoms before His own eternal kingdom. Therefore, the prophet extols his God as the one who sets up and deposes kings. The plurals at the end of **2:23** ("we" and "us") indicate that the other three young men of **chapter 1** are still taking part in this matter with Daniel.

Daniel's Humility before the King

1. The captain of the king's guard may have wished to take some credit for finding the one who could interpret the king's dream. At any rate his statement that Daniel is one of the Judean exiles is worth noting. Judah was a tiny country and an easy prey for mighty Babylon. Yet the theme of Nebuchadnezzar's dream was the fall of all the kingdoms of the earth (including Babylon) before the kingdom of the God of the people of Judah.

2. Daniel's disclaimer of being able to relate and interpret the king's dream by his own power even echoes the objection of the Babylonian wise men to the king's original demand. It is ironic that the wise men of Babylon considered their gods to be inaccessible **(2:11),** but the dream would be made known by the true God, who, though He is the "God in heaven" **(2:28),** is readily accessible to believers through prayer. Joseph acted in a similar way before the king of Egypt.

3. The expression "latter days" is almost a technical term in the Scriptures for the time of the coming of the age of salvation, which was fulfilled through the person and work of Jesus. The dream of the king revealed what was to take place between his own time and the coming of God's time of salvation.

The Dream Related

1. The poorer metals of which each successive portion of the statue was composed represent the gradual deterioration of the kingdoms of the world. This assertion stands over against any notion (whether of a liberal, a Marxist, a millennialist, or any other origin) that human effort can gradually improve the world.

2. The stone was not cut by human hands. This would be something of God's doing, without any contribution on the part of people. This is part of the background of the New Testament's description of Christ as the stone the builders rejected (e.g., **1 Peter 2:4–8**).

3. The stone struck the feet of the statue, indicating that this saving act of the "latter days" would take place at the end of this succession of kingdoms. The fact that the entire image was reduced to dust indicates that God's kingdom would overcome all the kingdoms of the earth.

The Dream Interpreted

1. The plural "we" of **2:36,** as well as the word "your" in **2:47** (which in the Aramaic is also plural), indicates that Daniel's three friends accompanied him.

2. The prophet noted that it was God who gave Nebuchadnezzar his kingdom, might, and glory and who caused him to have dominion over all his subjects. In this way Daniel indicated that it is the God of Judah who

sets up the kingdoms of the world and allows their rulers to have dominion.

In connection with this question, you will want to point out how Daniel's interpretation sets forth the biblical distinction between God's kingdom of grace (also called the kingdom of the right hand) and His kingdom of power (also called the kingdom of the left hand). The might and splendor of Nebuchadnezzar's empire (and, for that matter, of any earthly kingdom) was under the watchful eye of the God of Judah, who created the world and who continues to uphold and preserve it. One of the ways in which He does this is through government, which employs law and the controlled use of force to keep a degree of order in the world. Nevertheless, people's efforts to exalt themselves within the kingdom of power will come to naught, for the only lasting kingdom is God's kingdom of grace (symbolized in the dream by the stone), in which the Gospel of His grace is proclaimed that people might have salvation. The following diagram may be helpful in summarizing the distinction between these two kingdoms of God (you may wish to put this on the board):

Kingdom of the Left Hand	Kingdom of the Right Hand
1. Government is God's servant	1. Church is God's servant
2. Makes laws and keeps order	2. Proclaims the Word for salvation
3. Controlled use of force	3. Motivation of the Gospel
4. Obedience even compelled	4. Willing obedience
5. All humanity (creatures)	5. Believers (children)
6. Owed taxes, honor, and obedience within limits **(Acts 5:29)**	6. God owed faith, worship, and unlimited obedience
7. Public redress **(Acts 25:11)**	7. No revenge **(Romans 12:16–21)**
8. Temporal reach	8. Eternal reach

Critics have questioned the correctness of what is said here about the extent and splendor of Nebuchadnezzar's kingdom, since it was never as extensive as the Medo-Persian or Greek empires. But if the kingdom of Nebuchadnezzar is regarded as the continuation of the ancient empires of Babylon, this objection proves to be quite groundless.

3. In contrast to the kingdoms represented by the image, the kingdom of God is (1) established by God's grace without any involvement on the part of people **(2:34)**; (2) eternal and unchanging **(2:44)**; and (3) universal **(2:35**; the rock became a mountain that encompassed the whole world—even as God's salvation reaches out to all).

4. **Matthew 13:31–32**—the parable of the mustard seed teaches that God's kingdom encompasses the whole world (people from all over the world are symbolized by the birds of the air who find rest in the tree's

branches). **Mark 4:26–29**—the parable of the growing seed shows that God's kingdom does not depend on human effort (also shown in **John 18:36** and **1 Thessalonians 2:12**). **Hebrews 1:8; 12:28;** and **Revelation 11:15** indicate that God's kingdom is eternal and unchanging.

5. God's kingdom was established by the Lord Jesus.

The Aftermath of the Interpretation

1. Nebuchadnezzar was a polytheist, and the record of his behavior in the rest of the book of Daniel indicates that his praise of Daniel's God was not a conversion to faith in Him alone. Yet the demonstration of God's power was so great that it elicited this confession from the haughty despot. Daniel accepted this homage as directed not to him but to the God to whom he had given credit for revealing the dream and its interpretation. As he had promised, the king gave Daniel great honor and many gifts.

2. Since his friends had assisted him with their prayers and since (as **chapter 1** demonstrates) they were otherwise well qualified for service in the government, Daniel requested appointment for his friends Shadrach, Meshach, and Abednego.

The Word for Us

1. Participants may share insights as to how the things of the world may appear more attractive than the things of God.

2. A theme of this chapter is that God's ways are ultimately preferable to the ways of the world. We are members of His worldwide, eternal kingdom of grace through faith in Christ, and nothing the world offers can beat that.

Closing

Follow the suggestion in the study guide.

Lesson 4

The Three Men in the Fiery Furnace

The Class Session

Have volunteers read "Theme Verses," "Goal," and "What's Going On Here?"

Searching the Scriptures

Nebuchadnezzar's Golden Image

1. It seems that Nebuchadnezzar never fully understood the meaning of the various episodes recorded in Daniel. Therefore, the dream of **chapter 2** may have given him the idea of making an image of gold.

2. The passages here cited show that the huge statue need not have been of pure gold but could well have been made of some other material that was overlaid with the precious metal. Remarkable statues, some even taller than the one described in this chapter, are known to have existed in the ancient world.

3. Lying face down before someone is a position for worship frequently mentioned in the Scriptures. When the verb *worship* occurs in the Old Testament, it is often employed as a translation for a verb meaning to lie prostrate on the ground. Such a posture implies total submission to the one being worshiped.

4. This cruel form of punishment is also mentioned in other accounts from this part of the world.

The Accusation against the Three Judeans

1. The charges raised against the three young men were true. However, they were malicious because they were raised with a view toward evil. The accusations were made out of jealousy toward the three and with the thought that they would be deposed and others could take their place.

2. This verse clearly indicates that paying homage to the king's statue also involved acknowledging his gods. The three are confronted with the same situation they faced when they were first selected for service to the king.

3. The astrologers (literally, Chaldeans) accuse the three of ingratitude and indifference toward the king, who had appointed them to positions of authority and prestige.

The King Confronts the Three Young Men

1. By their suggestions that the three Judeans are ungrateful and disloyal, the Chaldeans are successful in arousing the king's rage against them.

2. Nebuchadnezzar may have suspected that the motives of the Chaldeans were self-serving. Perhaps he was favorably inclined toward the three on account of fruitful and faithful service that they, along with Daniel, had performed in his government. At any rate, he gives the three young men a second chance, probably thinking that when confronted by the king himself, they will conform to his decree.

3. The words of Nebuchadnezzar recorded in this verse amount to a

challenge against the God of Judah and incidentally supply further proof that the worship of his image was understood by all as an act of worship to his gods.

4. The term *ethical ability* is sometimes used to describe the reference in this verse to God's ability or inability to deliver the young men from the furnace of burning fire. Their answer does not mean that they questioned if their God had the power to save them but if it would be in accord with His purpose and good will for Him to spare them. The three young men show great faith. They will not deny the God of Judah, regardless of whether or not He delivers them from this particular hardship. Our Lord does not promise us an easy life, for we must bear our crosses, even as Christ suffered unjustly before receiving the glory of His resurrection (**1 Peter 2:20–25; 3:17–18**).

The Punishment Is Increased

1. The king's anger is described in **3:19.** As a result he ordered the furnace heated seven times hotter than normal. The furnace was probably similar to a modern limekiln, with an opening at the top for inserting the ore (or the victims) and a side opening at the bottom, through which the refined metal could be gathered and into which Nebuchadnezzar could peer. See **3:25–26. Daniel 3:22** also gives the impression that Nebuchadnezzar was in a hurry to see the punishment carried out.

2. Men of valor were needed for the task of throwing the Judeans into the fire (**3:20**). The fire was so hot that these men were killed (**3:22**).

3. The three men were cast into the furnace still bound. They were helpless, and as we will see in the next section, the Lord delivered them from their bonds.

The Miraculous Deliverance

1. Since the Lord had delivered the three young men from the forces of nature and the power of men by sending His angel, this canticle, which summons the forces of nature, angels, people in general, and especially the people of God to bless Him, became attached to this story from the book of Daniel.

2. Those who had been bound when they were cast into the fire were free and walking (apparently in a leisurely manner) in the midst of the fire. A "son of the gods" or "son of God" is a term sometimes used in the Old Testament for angels. See for example, **Job 1:6** and the NIV text note.

3. Nebuchadnezzar seems to have remained a polytheist to the very end. He was willing to call the God of Judah the Most High, but there is no indication that he acknowledged God to be the only God.

4. The extent of the miracle is seen by the successively greater evi-

dences given in this verse: the bodies of the three were not harmed; their hair was not singed; their clothing was not affected, and the smell of smoke could not even be detected. The various officials who were present examined them to verify the miracle.

Nebuchadnezzar's Decree

1. The king confessed that the God of Judah had overturned his command. He noted that the three young men had trusted in the Lord. This agrees with the statement in **Hebrews 11** that it was by faith that the three men had quenched (that is, been delivered from) the fire. Nebuchadnezzar's statement also indicated that the three young men had risked their lives rather than deny the Lord.

2. The king acknowledged that the God of the three Judeans was the only one who could deliver in such a manner. Nebuchadnezzar decreed the same punishment for those who slandered this God as he had for the wise men who had been unable to reveal his dream.

3. Nebuchadnezzar in some way gave the three a greater degree of responsibility, prestige, and/or prosperity as officials in his government than had been theirs prior to this event.

The Word for Us

1. Participants may share insights regarding the great potential for evil that lies in human speech, so that such speech is to have no place among Christians.

2. As time permits, let the class members apply the lessons of this chapter to everyday situations. Suffering of one type or another (ridicule, the loss of a job, and the like) will at times inflict the Christian who lives his or her life in accord with the will of God. Yet the Lord promises strength to endure and eternal life to those who are His. In this light we can see that it is a privilege to suffer for the sake of Christ **(Acts 5:41)**.

3. **Verse 12** of **1 Peter 4** ("fiery ordeal" RSV) is most likely an allusion to **Daniel 3.** Here the apostle makes it clear that Christians can expect to suffer for their faith. Yet such suffering is a privilege because it is a proof that one is a Christian who will be saved for eternal life.

Closing

Follow the suggestion in the study guide.

Lesson 5
Nebuchadnezzar's Madness

The Class Session

Have volunteers read "Theme Verse," "Goal," and "What's Going On Here?"

Searching the Scriptures

The Edict of Nebuchadnezzar

1. The reference to "peoples, nations and men of every language" indicates the importance that Nebuchadnezzar attached to the events he was about to relate. This grandiose style is also an example of the pride of the Babylonian rulers. The humbling of the pride of this world's rulers is the subject of this chapter.

2. Although we cannot say for certain, it seems that the king never did come to saving faith in the God of Judah. The exalted language he used here of Daniel's God may be due in part to the use of Daniel as an assistant in the composition of the edict.

Nebuchadnezzar's Dream

1. The prosperity of Nebuchadnezzar is noted in this verse, for from a human point of view his accomplishments gave him every reason to be proud. The message of this chapter concerns itself with the way in which the Lord opposes the proud of this world.

2. In view of the message of the dream of **chapter 2,** the king may well have feared that Daniel's interpretation of the dream would not be favorable to him. Therefore, he turned to him only when all other attempts at interpreting the dream had failed.

The Content of the Dream

1. For various reasons some students of the Scriptures, including conservative ones, feel that the Daniel mentioned in the book of Ezekiel is not the same person as the main character of the book of Daniel. The reasons for and against this identification are beyond the scope of this Bible study. Suffice it to say that the similarity of these verses is an argument in favor of such an identification.

2. The "world tree" is used in these passages as a symbol of something that encompasses the world. In the case of **Daniel 4** it refers to Nebuchadnezzar's control over much of the known world. In **Ezekiel 31** the world tree is used to deride the claims of power by Egypt. **Ezekiel 17** employs

this symbol to depict the universal significance of the return of the people of Israel to their homeland; a significance that can only be seen in light of the message of Mark where the world tree refers to the universal outreach of the kingdom of God, that is, of all that God does in the person and work of Jesus Christ to set up His rule of grace in, over, and among people.

3. This designation is used in **Daniel 4** (and nowhere else in Scripture) to refer to angels. The hymn of praise "Ye Watchers and Ye Holy Ones" makes use of this unique name for angels.

4. Since the reference to binding with a band of iron and bronze does not fit with the picture of the felling of the tree, it is possible that this part of the dream refers directly to some kind of bonds with which the king was held during his madness.

5. A comparison of **4:17** with **4:24** indicates that the decree of the watchers and holy ones was also the decree of the Most High. The thought may be here of the heavenly council of God, at which His angels are present and in which He determines the course of history. Since the angels are present at the heavenly council, they are privy to its decisions; therefore, what is in agreement with their decree has been strictly determined by the Lord **(Zechariah 3:1–7)**.

Daniel's Interpretation and Advice

1. Whereas the events foretold in the dream had a very direct message for Nebuchadnezzar, their message was also intended for all the living. We too are to learn from what is recorded here of how the Lord deals with the pride of people.

2. The term "heavens" (the plural is used in both the Aramaic of Daniel and the Greek of Matthew's gospel) served among the Jewish people of the latter part of the Old Testament era and of New Testament times as an identifier for the name of God.

3. Daniel's words were most likely to be understood of that which the Lutheran Confessions call "civil righteousness." His words had to do not with the way of salvation but with what was right in the civil realm. If Nebuchadnezzar would have become a good and upright ruler who looked out for the welfare of his subjects (rather than the proud and self-serving despot which, in general, the Babylonian kings proved themselves to be), then the Lord might have rewarded him in the civil realm and not inflicted him with the punishment foretold by his dream. It is possible that Daniel's words may have referred to the good works that follow saving faith, but this is much less likely. There is nothing in this verse to suggest that one could gain eternal salvation by doing such works. This verse offers an example of how necessary it is to distinguish between how God deals with

people in the civil realm (as His creatures) and the way in which He deals with us in the spiritual realm (depending on whether or not we are His children through faith in Jesus Christ).

Nebuchadnezzar's Madness

This statement of pride on the part of Nebuchadnezzar amounted to a challenge against the God of Judah, who had warned him against such pride in the dream he had experienced the previous year. It is worth noting that archaeologists have discovered inscriptions from Nebuchadnezzar's Babylon that include language very similar to that which is attributed to him here. From a worldly point of view Nebuchadnezzar accomplished some remarkable things as a builder, including the construction of the renowned hanging gardens of Babylon.

Nebuchadnezzar's Recovery

1. The point made by **4:34** is that the punishment had completed its purpose. The king's heavenward glance denoted his acknowledgment of the sovereignty of the Most High, and with his doing that his reason was restored to him.

2. This verse denotes that none—neither the inhabitants of earth (people) or heaven (the angels—"powers of heaven")—are beyond God's control.

3. Nebuchadnezzar's repentance is probably to be compared with the repentance of King Ahab. Neither was a repentance that also included saving faith. Nevertheless, by acknowledging their wrongdoing these two kings did obtain some earthly reward from the Lord.

The Word for Us

1. Adolph Hitler would be one such example.

2. Through study of these verses participants should come to see that the Holy Spirit works through the Gospel, strengthening faith so that we might possess Christlike humility.

3. Participants should come to realize that humility is an expression of love through faith in Christ Jesus. Both humility and love are practiced as they are shown toward others.

Closing

Follow the suggestion in the study guide.

Lesson 6
A Feast and a Den of Lions

The Class Session
Have volunteers read "Theme Verses," "Goal," and "What's Going On Here?"

Searching the Scriptures
Belshazzar's Feast

The accuracy of the data concerning Belshazzar given in **Daniel 5** has often been called into question by critics of the Old Testament. It is pointed out that Nebuchadnezzar, who died in 562 B.C., was succeeded by his son, who was succeeded by Nebuchadnezzar's son-in-law, who was succeeded by Nebuchadnezzar's grandson, who was succeeded by Nabonidus, who was unrelated by blood to Nebuchadnezzar and who was king of Babylon at the time of its fall to the Medes and Persians in 539. Belshazzar was never king of Babylon.

Many explanations of this information have been offered. The simplest is that Belshazzar shared a coregency with Nabonidus, who had married the mother of Belshazzar, this woman being the widow, the daughter-in-law, or the daughter of Nebuchadnezzar, thus making Belshazzar either the son or grandson of Nebuchadnezzar (which could be indicated by the Aramaic word *bar*, "son," which is used in **Daniel 5**).

Also, the terms *father* and *son* can be used in the Scriptures as synonyms for "ancestor" and "descendant," without denoting a biological father-son relationship. For instance, compare the genealogical listing in **Matthew 1:8** with the more complete one found in **1 Chronicles 3:11–12** (note that Uzziah = Azariah as may be seen from a comparison of **2 Kings 15:1–2** with **2 Chronicles 26:1–3**):
- **Matthew 1:8:** "Jehoram the father of Uzziah."
- **1 Chronicles 3:11–12:** "Jehoram his son, Ahaziah his son, Joash his son, Amaziah [Uzziah] his son."

A similar comparison can be made between **1 Chronicles 6:7,** where Meraioth is listed as the father of Amariah, and **Ezra 7:3,** where Amariah is listed as the son of Azariah who was the son of Meraioth.

Nabonidus is known from Babylonian historical records to have often been absent from the capital city on expeditions to rebuild temples of various gods. Belshazzar was left in charge of the ordinary affairs of the empire. Thus he was "the king," as he is called in the book of Daniel, in a popular sense, even though he was never formally the king of Babylon. Inscriptions bearing the name of Belshazzar have been found in ancient Babylon, and he is known from Babylonian records to have exercised the authority of the king. The lavish feast given by Belshazzar is not unlike the huge feasts given by other monarchs of the time as these are reported in Babylonian records.

The actions of Belshazzar and his guests were blasphemous. The vessels of the temple of God, intended for holy use, were profaned not only by common use but also by their use in acts of worship to pagan gods.

The Handwriting on the Wall

1. The Aramaic term rendered "third highest ruler" in many English translations of Daniel is thought by some (also some conservatives) to be a title of a position, so that it should be rendered by an English word such as "officer." If the term does mean "third highest ruler in the kingdom," this may be an additional piece of evidence for the fact that Belshazzar shared a coregency with Nabonidus, so that Belshazzar was the second highest ruler in the land and was therefore unable to give any higher office than "third highest ruler" to the one who would interpret the mysterious handwriting.

2. Since the wives of Belshazzar were already present at the banquet (**5:2**), it seems likely that the queen who is mentioned in **5:10** was the queen mother, perhaps either the widow, the daughter-in-law, or the daughter of Nebuchadnezzar, whom Nabonidus had married. This suggestion would account for her familiarity with the deeds of Daniel during the reign of Nebuchadnezzar.

Daniel's Summoning and Interpretation

1. Like the prophet Elisha, Daniel was no seeker of worldly gain. He was a seeker of truth who would not misuse the gift of God for his own reward but would offer the God-given interpretation without personal gain. His refusal may also have pointed to the coming interpretation: since Belshazzar's kingdom was about to fall, his rewards would not be worth accepting anyway.

2. **5:18–19** shows that the mighty Nebuchadnezzar enjoyed almost unrestricted power. Yet his power was given him by God. When Nebuchadnezzar would not humble himself before God, he was humiliated. Belshazzar could have learned from Nebuchadnezzar's experience to humble himself before God. Instead he "set [himself] up against the Lord of heaven" (**5:23**). Thus a much worse fate would befall Belshazzar, who, although he was less powerful than Nebuchadnezzar, was filled with greater pride.

3. The Old Testament contains these instances of polemic against all

other gods, who have no power. **Psalm 115:8; 135:18;** and **Isaiah 44:9, 18–20** say that those who worship idols are like the things they worship; they amount to nothing and have no spiritual understanding or knowledge.

4. The interpretation involves a number of wordplays. The days of Belshazzar's reign had been numbered (*mene* means "numbered") by God and brought to an end. Belshazzar had been weighed (*tekel* means "weighed") in the scales and found wanting. The Aramaic word *mene* can also be a monetary unit (a mina [see **Luke 19:13**]). The Aramaic word *tekel* can also refer to a unit of weight and hence of money (a shekel [see **Genesis 23:14–16**]). Belshazzar's kingdom would be divided and given to the Medes and Persians. The Aramaic word for "divided" *(peres)*, especially in the plural (which occurs in **verse 25**), can refer to a half unit of weight or monetary value, such as a half a mina or more probably a half a shekel. In the singular this term is almost identical to the Aramaic word for "Persia" or "Persians."

The fact that the Medes are listed first in **5:28** is in keeping with the fact that the Medes arose to prominence before the Persians, eventually to be united with the latter before being surpassed by them. The play on words of *peres* and Persians also indicates the supremacy of the Persians and the fact that Daniel knew that separate empires of the Medes and Persians had never existed (an issue that will come up in future lessons when we discuss the four world empires).

The Aftermath

From other historical documents of the time we learn that the fall of Babylon to the Medes and Persians did not involve a long or bloody conflict. The Babylonians did not care much for the rule of Nabonidus, believing him to have neglected the worship of their gods. Cyrus, the ruler of the Medes and Persians, took the city of Babylon without a fight in 539 B.C. He rechanneled the waters of the Euphrates River so that his troops could easily enter the city, whose residents welcomed him as a liberator. Such is the way in which the Lord carried out the judgment he had foretold by the handwriting on the wall.

The Plot against Daniel

1. Sources from the reign of Cyrus indicate that Gobryas, serving under Cyrus as ruler of Babylon, appointed governors in Babylon during his reign. If the identification of Darius the Mede with this Gobryas is correct, this would provide a bit of confirmation of what is written in **Daniel 6:1.**

2. The Lord had given Daniel many exceptional qualities and gifts that suited him for the job. In addition to his wisdom and intellectual gifts, he was trustworthy and not corrupt or negligent. These gifts and qualities

enabled Daniel to survive the change in rulers. Daniel began his service to Nebuchadnezzar about 604 B.C. and served until after the fall of Babylon to Cyrus in 539 (see **Daniel 10:1**), meaning that his career lasted more than 65 years.

3. Daniel's enemies lied when they presented their proposal as having the backing of all the governors whom Darius had appointed. Daniel of course had not agreed to their proposal. Their objective was to forbid all prayers, except those offered to Darius, for a 30-day period, for they realized that only in this way would they be able to find any criminal offense in Daniel, of whom they were jealous and whom they wished to depose. Since ancient kings were often thought to be lesser deities and even the sons of the chief gods, this proposal would not have appeared outlandish to a pagan ruler like Darius. Apparently he was sufficiently flattered to give his approval.

4. Extrabiblical sources also confirm the practice of the Medes and Persians that their laws and royal decrees were irrevocable.

The Consequences of Daniel's Courage

1. An open-air room as a place for prayer is mentioned or suggested in a few biblical passages. The fact that Daniel prayed three times a day indicates the value of setting aside appointed times for prayer as a wholesome discipline for the child of God.

2. Christians are to be good citizens of the state, rendering to Caesar the things that are Caesar's and to God the things that are God's **(Mark 12:13–17)**. One of the things that we are not to render to Caesar, however, is worship, for this is due only to God. Should any government attempt to compel such worship to itself (or to anything other than the true God), believers must follow the example of Daniel and of the apostles and obey God rather than people. This also applies to any action the state may require of us that goes against what we know to be the will of God.

3. With their reference to the fact that Daniel was one of the Judean exiles, his opponents were intimating that he was an ungrateful and disloyal foreigner. They openly charged him with paying no attention to the king.

Daniel in the Lions' Den

1. The word *innocent* or *blameless* means that in violating this particular decree Daniel had done right in the sight of God; therefore, the Lord vindicated his innocence. The real cause of Daniel's deliverance was the Lord, who delivered His faithful follower Daniel to show that Daniel's God and no other is God. The power of the Lord's angel is seen in stopping the lions, which in the ordinary course of things would have devoured Daniel (see question 3).

2. Daniel's trust or faith in the Lord and not any merit on his part was

the reason for his deliverance.

3. That the lions destroyed Daniel's opponents before their bodies even hit the floor of the lions' den is a further indication of the miraculous nature of the Lord's deliverance of His faithful one. The casting of these to the lions was also a justly deserved punishment for their attempt to have Daniel unfairly put to death. Sources from the ancient world inform us that it was a Persian custom to execute also the immediate family of anyone found guilty of a capital offense.

The Decree of the King

1. Darius remained a polytheist, just as Nebuchadnezzar had been. His edict required only that the people of the land give reverence to the God of Daniel, just as they had once rendered it to Nebuchadnezzar. Nothing is intimated about the Lord being the only God. The profoundly religious and exalted language of the decree of Darius may be due to the influence of Daniel helping the king to compose the edict.

2. This chapter illustrates the theme of the great reversal that the Lord may effect for His people.

The Word for Us

1. Babylon was such a great enemy of the people of God in the Old Testament that in the entire Bible it is often used as a symbol for all powers that are hostile to God. Yet such evil will fall, and Christ will exalt His people to eternal life in heaven.

2. Christians will face opposition from the world on account of their Christian faith and way of life. Yet it is worthwhile to remain faithful to our Lord Jesus Christ, for He will deliver us and bring us to eternal life. Such faithfulness in teaching, in witness, and in Christian living is that to which God's people are called.

3. Christ not only gives us the finest example of faithfulness during suffering, His suffering is the only way to our eternal life. This encourages us in our own suffering, for even as our Lord suffered unjustly, we may also expect to suffer for our Christian faith. Nevertheless, as He rose victorious for our salvation, He will deliver us from our sufferings to eternal glory.

4. The Lord has power over those who would oppose and ridicule Him and His people. Ultimately His will be the victory.

Closing

Follow the suggestion in the study guide.

Lesson 7
The Son of Man

The Class Session
Have volunteers read "Theme Verses," "Goal," and "What's Going On Here?"

Searching the Scriptures
Daniel's Dream and Visions

1. The specific mention of the four winds seems to indicate that the beasts that arise from the sea represent all of the powers of the world.

2. The sea is an ancient symbol of chaos and evil, so used in the Old Testament and in the religious myths of ancient paganism. The beasts rise from the sea because they represent the powers of this fallen world as they are set in rebellion against God. These will be no more in heaven; hence **Revelation** says that in heaven there will be no more sea. The beasts symbolize kingdoms of the world, which is corrupted by evil; hence, these kingdoms themselves are characterized by evil.

3. The name and description of God the Father gives an aura of both dignity (in contrast to the beasts) and eternity. The color white is here a symbol of holiness. It is also interesting to note that when the designation "the Most High" is used throughout this chapter, it occurs in a plural form. This use of the plural is usually called the "plural of majesty" (something like the practice of a king referring to himself as "we") and adds to the picture of splendor that belongs to God.

4. The "one like a son of man" comes with the clouds, which are the "chariot" of God and associated with the heavens, the "abode" of God. This is in contrast with the sea (chaos and evil) as the origin of the beasts. This last figure is human in appearance; this denotes a dignified status over against the uncivilized savagery of that which is symbolized by the beasts.

5. The authority, glory, and sovereign power given to the one like a son of man, as well as the worship He received from all peoples, is reflected in the heavenly hymn of praise in **Revelation 5** (upon which the canticle "Worthy Is Christ" is based). The kingdom and dominion of this one is said to extend to all peoples, nations, and tongues and to be everlasting. Note the common conclusion to the Lord's Prayer, where we confess that this authority, glory, and sovereign power belongs to God for ever and ever.

6. It is commonly asserted in critical circles that the one like a son of man is symbolic only of the saints of the Most High. Not only does this fly

in the face of our Lord's explicit identification of Himself as the Son of man, but it also overlooks the biblical concept of corporate personality. Christ so closely identifies Himself (by Baptism and the Gospel and through faith) with His people that what is true of Him also becomes true of them. Thus it can be stated that dominion and a kingdom was given both to the individual described as one like a son of man (who was the preincarnate Christ) and to the saints of the Most High.

7. The kingdom and dominion of the Son of Man and of His saints lasts forever, in contrast to the kingdoms of this world, which all pass away.

Jesus' Use of the Title *Son of Man*

Ask various class members to take turns reading the paragraphs under this section. Also look up the biblical references listed within the paragraphs in order to get an appreciation for the way in which our Lord incorporated many of the major messianic concepts of the Old Testament under the sole title "Son of man." In connection with point 4, you may find it helpful to point out that in a book called Enoch, which was probably familiar to most Jewish people at Jesus' time, the term *Son of man* is used extensively, and there the Son of Man is also identified with the Messiah. This helped our Lord to be able to teach others that He was indeed the Messiah without causing them to think that He had come for the purpose of leading a revolt against Rome (a common misconception about the Messiah in New Testament times). Then lead the class in looking up the references listed and matching them with the correct use of the term *Son of man*. You might want to divide the passages among class members and have them read their assigned passages aloud.

Matthew 8:20—humility; **Matthew 12:40**—passion prediction; **Matthew 13:37**—reveals God; **Matthew 16:28**—equality with God; **Mark 2:10**—divine authority; **Mark 8:31**—passion prediction; **Mark 10:45**—passion prediction; **Mark 14:62**—the Second Coming; **Luke 6:5**—divine authority; **Luke 12:40**—the Second Coming; **Luke 19:10**—messianic King; **John 1:51**—reveals God; **John 6:62**—equality with God; **John 12:23, 32, 34**—messianic King.

A Scene of Judgment

1. The angels are here represented as being attendants in the divine throne room at this scene of judgment. This recalls the fact that when the Son of man comes for the final judgment, His angels will accompany Him.

2. The books in this scene of judgment are records of all the deeds of people, in this context specifically the deeds of the four beasts and the little horn.

3. This picture of judgment depicts not only the final judgment but also

the biblical doctrine of justification. According to this doctrine those who have faith in Christ are judged "not guilty" in the heavenly courtroom by virtue of the fact that the righteous obedience of Christ is reckoned, or credited, to their account so that their sins are forgiven and they are righteous and innocent in the eyes of the Judge.

The Word for Us

1. Participants should note how Christ attained to glory by way of His humility. The discussion on this question may well lead into the following one.

2. Strong is the inclination for a feel-good religion or a theology of success or self-help. The Scriptures, on the other hand, show us that following after God's way in Christ may well bring hardship or disadvantage in this life. Nevertheless, the ultimate outcome of God's way is infinitely superior to anything offered us by worldly or human means.

3. We see here the value of the Son of man, even in His lowliness, over the things of this world. We give Him priority over all other things, in spite of the apparent advantages others may seem to offer.

4. Participants may share the particular strength they themselves have received from this lesson.

Closing

Follow the suggestion in the study guide.

Lesson 8
God's Kingdom and World Kingdoms

The Class Session

Have volunteers read "Theme Verse," "Goal," and "What's Going On Here?"

Searching the Scriptures
The Four World Empires

1. Both the lion and the eagle were employed as symbols for the Babylonian empire of Nebuchadnezzar. The experience of Nebuchadnezzar is reflected in the description of this beast being transformed into a man.

Archaeological excavations have uncovered a winged lion (with a man's head) from ancient Babylon.

2. The empire of the Medes and Persians, voracious in its conquests, is symbolized by the bear. Its being raised up on one side is surely a reference to the two nationalities that made up this empire and to the fact that the Persians were by far the more dominant. The swiftness with which Alexander the Great conquered his empire is probably the meaning of the speedy leopard appearing as a symbol for this empire. The four wings and four heads reflect the ultimate division of Alexander's empire into four parts after his death. The evidence of the book of Daniel is that the author never conceived of the separate existence of a Median empire apart from that of the Medes and Persians.

3. The fourth empire of **Daniel 2** and **7** is to be identified with Rome. Some wish to identify the second, third, and fourth empires of these chapters as the empires of the Medes, Persians, and Greeks. They do so because they think that Daniel was written after the breakup of Alexander's empire but before the rise of Rome. And they do not think it possible that Daniel could have predicted the rise of the Greek Empire (if Daniel was written at the time it claims to have been written) or the Roman Empire in advance.

Conservative scholars, who believe in the possibility of predictive prophecy in the Scriptures and who identify the second and third kingdoms respectively as Medo-Persia and Greece, generally identify the fourth empire as Rome, since Rome was the next great world empire after the breakup of the empire of Alexander. The fact that **Daniel 2:44–45** indicates that the fourth empire will be in power when the kingdom of God arises through the coming of the messianic stone, that is, of Christ, is another argument for identifying the fourth world empire with Rome. The great military power of the Romans is aptly depicted by the iron metal of the great statue and the crushing power of the beast that was unlike any of the other beasts.

4. Belshazzar was the last "king" of the Babylonian Empire. Therefore, it was fitting for Daniel to note that this dream, which foretold the fall of all the empires of the world before the kingdom of God, took place during his reign. Despite the apparent power of Babylon, it—along with the empires that would succeed it—would surely fall, while the kingdom of the Ancient of Days and one like a son of man would endure.

5. The empires of people have their origin in the world. The kingdom of the Son of man is not of this world. Not only is it different in character from the outward splendor of this world's kingdoms (seeming to be inferior when judged by outward appearances, but in fact being far greater in

glory), but it is also a kingdom that will overcome and surpass the kingdoms of this world.

6. The little horn of Daniel 7 is a symbol (as is the beast of **Revelation 13**) for all that is reckoned under the name "Antichrist." Antichrist speaks great things against God and His people, and for a time he prevails over them. This indicates that the times just prior to the end will be very bad for the saints (contrary to the assertions of some forms of millennialism, which teach that things will get better and better for the people of God in the days preceding the final judgment). The numbers 10 and 3 probably refer simply to kings and leaders in general and have no specific reference. That this is the case is most strongly suggested by the fact that the 10 horns arise all at once and not one after another in succession. The meaning is that Antichrist will use anything at its disposal, even government, in its war against God and His saints. But the ultimate victory belongs to the Ancient of Days, and the Antichrist will be destroyed and thrown into the blazing fire.

7. The presence of an angel to interpret the visions received is a standard feature of apocalyptic literature. Whenever such an angel is identified by name in the book of Daniel, he is always called Gabriel, the same angel who announced the birth of Christ to Mary. Since the prophet who received such angelic guidance was troubled by this vision, we should not feel disappointed at our inability to know all that is meant by this portion of the Scriptures.

8. The Lord intervenes to deliver His people and to give them a kingdom. Since the kingdom is the possession of the one like a son of man, we can see that our deliverance and eternal kingdom is given to us through Him. And the one like a son of man is He who used the title "Son of man" to foretell His suffering, death, and resurrection.

The Kingdom of God

Have volunteers read the paragraphs in the study guide and also the biblical references.

1. The kingdom comes to us as a gift of grace (**Luke 12:32**), and it comes to us only for the sake of Jesus Christ (**Luke 11:20**). **Daniel 7:22** indicates that the kingdom is given to the saints of the Most High.

2. Gabriel told Mary that Jesus would be the promised King from David's line (i.e., the Messiah) who would rule over the kingdom of God.

3. **Matthew 16** recounts one of two occasions (the other being reported in **John 20:19–23**) when our Lord gave to His church the authority to forgive sins. See also **Matthew 18:15–18**. The reference in **Matthew 16** to this being the keys of the kingdom indicates that it is through the forgiveness of sins given by Christ through His church's ministry of Word and

Sacrament that one is given the kingdom of God.

4. The son of this parable represents Christ, who was unjustly put to death while coming to establish the kingdom, the reign of God. **Matthew 21:42** alludes to His resurrection. After telling this parable, Jesus noted that because the Jewish religious leaders **(Matthew 21:45)** rejected Him, the kingdom would be taken from them and given to those who would produce fruit in keeping with it.

5. The lowly beginnings of the kingdom of God are symbolized by the mustard seed, here referred to as the smallest of all seeds. **Daniel 7** indicates that Antichrist prevails over the saints for a time, but in the end they receive dominion and a kingdom.

6. Both of these parables indicate that God and His kingdom must be revealed to us by Christ through the Word (here symbolized by the seed).

7. **Daniel 7:14** indicates that the kingdom of the Son of man will embrace those from all peoples, nations, and languages. Even as yeast affects an entire lump of dough, so the kingdom of God is universal in its scope.

8. **Matthew 13** describes the kingdom of God as a kingdom that has eternal glory as its goal and outside of which there is only judgment. **Daniel 7** describes the judgment that comes upon the enemies of God's people as well as the victory and glory that will be given His saints.

The Word for Us

1. The kingdoms of the world often appear preferable (more powerful, more wealthy) to God's kingdom. In truth, despite whatever it costs to be allied with it, the kingdom of God is superior.

2. Even the best of the world's kingdoms are corrupted by sin. God's kingdom in Christ is the only thing with eternal value.

3. Participants may share their own insights as to how the message of this chapter, including that regarding the Son of Man studied in the previous lesson, strengthens them for putting their faith in Christ.

Closing

Follow the suggestion in the study guide.

Lesson 9

The Ram and the He-Goat

The Class Session

Have volunteers read "Theme Verse," "Goal," and "What's Going On Here?"

Searching the Scriptures

The Circumstances of the Vision

1. Since Susa was the capital of the empire of the Medes and Persians, which would be the next empire to assume control of the ancient Near East, it was fitting that this city should have been the locale of Daniel's vision.

2. A comparison with the statements of Ezekiel and John strongly suggests that Daniel was not physically present in Susa but was there only in his vision.

3. Use this exercise to review the content of Daniel's vision. Note especially the two horns of unequal size on the ram and the goat's one horn which was broken into four other horns, out of which a little horn grew. Defer answering questions regarding the interpretation of the vision until the next section of this lesson.

4. We are told that the angels, even though they themselves have no need of it, are interested in peering into the story and circumstances of humanity's salvation.

The Vision Interpreted

1. In order that the vision Daniel had seen might be interpreted for him, God (for He was apparently the one whose voice was heard) sent the angel Gabriel to interpret the vision. Gabriel was of course also the messenger who announced the birth of John the Baptizer to his father and of Christ to the Virgin Mary.

2. Daniel's panic and swoon was similar to the reactions of other biblical characters who found themselves in the presence of God. Sinful people cannot stand in the presence of almighty God and survive, for His holiness will destroy sinners. Since His angels are also holy, Daniel was frightened being in the presence of one of them. This verse is another indication of our sinfulness and inability to come before God apart from Jesus Christ. The angels are sent by God to serve His people, and so the angel Gabriel served Daniel by reviving him from his deep sleep.

3. The ram with two horns symbolized the empire of the Medes and Persians. This symbolism clearly indicates that the author of Daniel did not think that there had ever been separate Median and Persian empires. Although the Medes arose to prominence before the Persians, the Persians far surpassed the Medes in this empire as was symbolized by the second of the ram's two horns becoming the dominant one.

4. The three directions mentioned here correspond to the three directions in which the empire of the Medes and Persians advanced in its conquests. These three directions may possibly be symbolized by the three ribs in the bear's mouth mentioned in **Daniel 7:5.** All the kingdoms of the world are symbolized in **Daniel 8** by beasts since all the kingdoms of the world are equally set in opposition against God. That no beast could stand before the ram depicts the repeated conquests of other nations by the Medes and Persians.

5. Alexander the Great is symbolized by the one large horn of the goat, which symbolizes Greece. He came from the west to conquer much of the then-known world. The great speed with which his conquests were accomplished is symbolized by the fact that the goat came without even touching the ground. The goat's crossing of the whole earth refers to the worldwide extent of Alexander's conquests. The anger exhibited by the goat toward the ram may reflect the Greeks' desire for revenge against the Medes and Persians, since the latter had often tried (unsuccessfully) to conquer Greece. Even as the goat destroyed the ram, so Alexander destroyed the empire of the Medes and Persians.

6. The beautiful land is a reference to Israel.

7. The host of the heavens (in this case a synonym for the stars) serves as a symbol for the people of God, who were oppressed and persecuted by Antiochus.

8. Antiochus called himself "Epiphanes," which amounted to a virtual claim of being an earthly manifestation of one of the gods. Thus he set himself in direct opposition to God. The Jews whom he persecuted, making use of a clever play on words, called him "Epimanes," that is, "madman." Antiochus wished to spread the culture and religion of Greece throughout his realm, and so he outlawed the historic faith of God's people. **1 Maccabees 1** reports how Antiochus endeavored to do this. He proclaimed that everyone in his domain was to worship his gods. He banned the temple sacrifices and other religious rites of the Jewish people. He forbade the study of the Hebrew Scriptures and the practice of circumcision. He turned the Jerusalem temple into a shrine for the worship of the Olympian Zeus (which was more or less identified with the ancient Canaanite god Baal), so that swine's flesh was sacrificed on the high altar, and the orgias-

tic worship rituals of this god were carried on in the temple precincts. Those who would not obey his orders were to be put to death. It is reported that women who had had their infant sons circumcised were executed with their babies hung around their necks.

The Comfort in the Vision

1. It was not by the efforts of people (literally "by no hand"), but by God's intervention that Antiochus was overthrown. **1 Maccabees 6:8–16** reports how he became grievously ill and died.

2. The 2,300 days do not correspond to any historical period. Explanations that seek to identify these days with a period during the persecutions of Antiochus IV, such as by reckoning the 2,300 evenings/mornings as equaling 1,150 days, do not fit well with the historical facts and hence are not convincing. Instead, they are a symbol, for they designate a period of a little less than seven years, seven being a number of completeness. The dominion of Antiochus (and indeed of all evil directed against the people of God) has its day, but its time is limited. It will not even attain to one complete period of time before God brings it to an end.

3. The atrocities of Antiochus are typical of the evil that will befall the people of God prior to the end. The last days will be times of trial for God's people, yet even as He overthrew Antiochus, so God will deliver His people from the evil of the latter days.

4. Jesus Christ is our only hope for deliverance. His deliverance is like that spoken of in **Daniel 8:25,** for it is a deliverance not by human power but solely by divine intervention. This encourages us to remain faithful to Him.

The Conclusion of the Vision

Even as the disciples of Jesus found His predictions of His redemptive work hard to understand, so Daniel had the same experience with his vision. For all of us it is necessary that the Holy Spirit open both our hearts and minds to hear what His Word says to us.

The Word for Us

1. Class members can share thoughts on the encouragement of knowing that even in spite of persecution, the Lord will deliver His people. No matter how sorely the world may persecute us, our God will deliver us in triumph.

2. Nazi Germany, the former Soviet Union, and Communist China are three examples that might be mentioned. God as Creator and Preserver may topple regimes such as these in this life, but even if He does not, He will surely judge the evil and deliver the believing in the life to come.

3. The word *crisis* derives from the Greek word for judgment, *krisis*. That being the case, someone has observed that every crisis is a dress rehearsal for the final *krisis*. As we are faithful to the Lord Christ in every crisis of opposition or hardship, we are preparing for the final *krisis*, when He will take His faithful people to life eternal.

Closing

Follow the suggestion in the study guide.

Lesson 10
Daniel's Prayer

The Class Session

Have volunteers read "Theme Verse," "Goal," and "What's Going On Here?"

Searching the Scriptures

The Setting of the Prayer

1. Briefly review what was said about this individual in lesson 6. Some scholars identify him with a subordinate of Cyrus who ruled over nothing more than the territory immediately adjacent to the city of Babylon. The passive form of the Hebrew verb used in **Daniel 9:1** ("was made ruler") could indicate that the author of Daniel did not think that this Darius was ever ruler over all the empire of the Medes and Persians.

2. Daniel was studying the prophecy of Jeremiah, through whom God had promised His people that He would return them to their land after 70 years. As a multiple of two numbers denoting completeness (7 and 10), 70 in these passages indicates that the exile would last until God's purposes were completed. It is worth noting that if Daniel, who had received such marvelous visions and who had the ability to interpret the dreams of others, studied the Scriptures that were written prior to his time, surely we should make ourselves students of the Scriptures.

3. Fasting, sackcloth, and ashes are ancient signs of repentance and are still used in connection with Ash Wednesday and other penitential times in the church year. Daniel's prayer was largely a prayer of repentance, hence the rationale for his penitential actions.

Daniel's Prayer: The Confession

1. Daniel was bold to offer his prayer to the Lord because the faith God had provided Him. Although He punished the guilty, He was also the one who kept the covenant He made with the people of Israel at Mount Sinai, after He claimed them as His own in the Exodus. Daniel could trust that the Lord would give ear to his pleas on behalf of the covenant people because the Lord kept the covenant He made with Israel, promising that they would be His people and that He would be their God.

2. Daniel confessed that the people had sinned, done wrong, been wicked, rebelled, and turned away from God's commands and laws.

3. Daniel also confessed that the people had ignored the very word of God, given through the prophets.

4. No Israelite (not even Daniel) could claim innocence of the sin that finally led the Lord to give the nation over into exile. The Babylonians did leave in the land of Judah the poor people, such as Jeremiah. These and their descendants would be those who were near, while those who were far off would refer to those carried off into exile.

5. The mercy of God, on account of which He would forgive the people of Israel, was their only hope for being delivered from His punishment.

6. When the Lord made His covenant with Israel, He warned the people that if they disobeyed His will, He would punish them, and their punishment would include exile in a foreign nation. The exile was a part of the curse that fell upon Israel for breaking the covenant. Yet because the Lord always kept His obligations with respect to the covenant, Daniel could come to the Lord with the hope of forgiveness.

7. The prophet also confessed that even though Israel had been in captivity for many years, by and large the people had not repented of the evil they had done to cause the exile.

8. These verses make the point that Israel could not blame the Lord for their captivity. The Lord was righteous in exiling them; the Israelites themselves were to blame for their plight.

Daniel's Prayer: The Petition

1. Just as Daniel rooted his prayer in the covenant the Lord had made after bringing Israel out of Egypt, so he grounded his petition in God's act of mercy in the exodus from Egypt. The "mighty hand" of God is a common anthropomorphism in the Old Testament and often recalls the mighty acts (such as the 10 plagues and the crossing of the Red Sea) by which the Lord brought Israel out of Egypt. In this way the Lord made a name for Himself as the God of Israel who delivers His people.

2. It was because of His righteousness, that is, His acts of making people

to be righteous or just in His sight, that He was the Savior of people.

3. A shining face is a symbol of favor and goodwill. The Lord makes His face shine on people not on account of anything in them but solely for His own sake, that is, out of His grace. The result of all of this would be that at the end of the appointed time He would allow the Israelites to return to their homeland.

4. Saying that Jerusalem was the place called by the Lord's name was another way of indicating that Jerusalem (particularly the temple) was the place in the Old Testament where God's grace was to be found. He did all this out of His mercy, the same mercy that moved Him to send Christ for our salvation and that moves Him to bring each of us into a saving relationship with Christ.

5. The Lord would allow Israel to return to its homeland solely because He had forgiven His people for their sins against His law.

6. Daniel prayed on the basis of the fact that the Lord Himself had blessed the people of Israel.

Gabriel's Arrival with the Lord's Answer

1. The omniscient Lord of all knows our requests before we put them into words. Therefore, He is able to answer our prayers before we speak them.

2. The time of the evening sacrifice was a common time of day for prayer among God's Old Testament people. Daniel followed this practice even though the temple was not standing at that time, which meant that the evening sacrifice could not be offered. He thereby showed his faithfulness to the God who had instituted the evening sacrifice as a way of properly worshiping Him. The practice of regular, set times for prayer is something every Christian would do well to establish for herself or himself.

3. Gabriel announced that he had been sent by God to impart wisdom and understanding to Daniel. The answer consisted of the mysterious prophecy of the 70 "sevens," recorded in **Daniel 9:24–27.**

The Word for Us

1. **Daniel 9:19** has been called the "Kyrie, eleison" ("Lord, have mercy") of the Old Testament. Like Daniel we too confess our faults, and we look for forgiveness, not because of how sorry we feel or how determined we are to amend our lives or anything else in ourselves, but only because of God's promises to forgive and His acts for our salvation accomplished by Jesus' death on the cross.

2. The only real solution to guilt is confessing it to God and receiving the assurance of His forgiveness for the sake of Christ.

Closing

Follow the suggestion in the study guide.

Lesson 11

The Prophecy of the 70 "Sevens"

The Class Session

Have volunteers read "Theme Verse," "Goal," and "What's Going On Here?"

Searching the Scriptures

The Prophecy in Overview

1. Keeping in mind the context described in **9:20–23,** students may find evidence of all five characteristics of apocalyptic literature listed in lesson 1. Especially prominent in **9:24–27** is the fifth characteristic: symbolism. In these verses we see the description of a "cosmic calendar" of events leading up to a watershed occurrence and the use of symbolic numbers.

2. Our Lord Himself clearly stated that it is impossible for mortals to know in advance the time of His final coming. Therefore, we must be on our guard, lest we attempt to misuse this portion of Scripture in order to compute the time of the end of the world.

The Benefits of the Seventy "Sevens"

1. Daniel's people, the people of Israel, and his holy city, Jerusalem, designated the people of God of the Old Testament era. The successor to Israel of old as God's people is the Christian church. Therefore, the promises of **Daniel 9** rightly apply to believers of all ages.

2. Although the expression "to bring an end to rebellion" might imply destroying those who commit transgression and the phrase "to seal up sin" could mean reserve it for judgment, it is more likely that all three expressions are synonymous ways of describing the forgiveness of sins. The three Hebrew words used here are the three major Old Testament words for sin. The reference to making atonement for iniquity recalls the importance in the Old Testament of the Day of Atonement. The book of Hebrews explains that the single death of Christ has replaced the yearly Day of Atonement as the means by which God gives to people the forgiveness of

their sins.

3. Righteousness ("justification" is another English term that renders the same biblical concept) is a major biblical term for what God does for humanity's salvation. By ourselves we are not righteous before God. Therefore, the righteous Christ died in our place that we might have such righteousness. If one is thereby righteous before God, he or she has eternal life. Thus **Daniel 9:24** describes this righteousness as being eternal.

4. "Vision and prophecy" would be sealed up because they would be fulfilled by Christ.

5. The concept of anointing also plays a prominent role in the following verse **(9:25)**. Since Christ has replaced the temple, whose innermost portion was called the Most Holy Place, as the place where God meets people in grace (through the forgiveness of sins), and since He now meets people in grace through the church's ministry of Word and Sacrament (hence the church is also designated as the temple of God), Christ is the anointed one who is mentioned in **verse 24** regardless of what is the correct translation of the end of the verse.

The "Sevens" of Blessing

1. The decree of Cyrus, king of Persia, that allowed the people of Judah to return to their homeland and to rebuild the temple of the Lord (which would of necessity have also entailed rebuilding the city of Jerusalem) is the only historical event that can be designated by this verse. The decree of Cyrus was issued in 538.

2. Ultimately this word to rebuild Jerusalem came forth from God Himself. He used Cyrus as His instrument to make it possible for His people to return to their homeland. This event marked the beginning of the divinely ordained period of 70 "sevens" which is here described.

3. In the Old Testament prophets, priests, and kings were anointed before assuming the tasks of their office. Since Jesus Christ holds the threefold office of prophet **(Luke 4)**, priest **(Hebrews 4)**, and king **(Luke 1)**, He is the one whose coming is foretold in **Daniel 9:25.**

4. If interpretation C is correct, the rebuilding of Jerusalem (referred to in both the first and last parts of **9:25**) is that which was accomplished by Nehemiah in about 445 B.C. If interpretation D is correct, the rebuilding of Jerusalem referred to in the last part of the verse refers to the building of the church of our Lord Jesus Christ. The rebuilding of Jerusalem referred to in the first part of the verse would still refer to the rebuilding done by Nehemiah. The reference to "plaza and moat" indicates a complete rebuilding of the city, either the literal city of Jerusalem (interpretation C) or the church, which lacks nothing because of Christ (interpretation D).

5. The troubled times to which this verse refers describe either the harassment that Nehemiah endured (interpretation C) or the afflictions that the church of God on earth must constantly bear (interpretation D).

The End of the 69th "Seven"

1. It seems quite natural to refer the cutting off of the anointed one to the death of Christ. However, if interpretation D is the correct one, it is not at all difficult to see this portion of the verse as a reference to the general apostasy of the last times, when faith in Christ is greatly minimized.

2. According to interpretation C the second prince is a symbol for the Romans, who destroyed the Jerusalem temple in A.D. 70. According to interpretation D this is a reference to Antichrist, which is everything that sets itself up over, against, and in place of Christ.

3. Jesus stated that there would be wars and conflict between nations until the end of the world.

4. The flood of **Daniel 9:26** recalls the destruction of the armies of Pharaoh at the time of the Exodus. Since Pharaoh is one of the Bible's earliest examples of an antichrist, this may be a way of saying that Antichrist will be destroyed by God, working for the good of His people with the same power He used to deliver His people at the time of the Exodus. Interpretation D would be most in harmony with this understanding of this portion of the verse.

The 70th "Seven"

1. According to interpretation C sacrifice and offering come to an end because they have been superseded and thus rendered unnecessary by the death of Christ. Thus with the destruction of the Jerusalem temple (at the end of the 70th "seven") these come to an end. According to interpretation D this refers to Antichrist opposing the true worship of God by His people **(2 Thessalonians 2:3–4),** who throughout the New Testament era offer Him spiritual sacrifices **(1 Peter 2:5).**

2. Interpretation C refers this to the temple, which is desolate because of the false worship that went on there after the death of Christ. This understanding of this word ("desolate" instead of "one who makes desolate") does not seem to be the most natural understanding of the Hebrew term used here. Interpretation D sees this as a reference to the victory of Christ over Antichrist, which will take place at the end, at a time ordained by God. Our Lord's reference to "the abomination that causes desolation" spoken of by Daniel **(Matthew 24:15)** seems to presuppose that which defiles true worship coming some time after His death. This would be another argument in favor of interpretation D. You may wish to mention that we will have more to say about "the abomination that causes desola-

tion" in the last lesson (in connection with its mention in **Daniel 11:31**).

Further Considerations

1. Since the vision itself does not give us a clue as to when the 70 "sevens" might come to an end, Christians should heed this fact and not attempt to use this (or any part of Scripture) in order to attempt to calculate the end of the world.

2. Both Antiochus and Antichrist oppose the true worship of God, and both are brought to naught by the power of God.

The Word for Us

1. Jesus Christ is at the center of the entire Scriptures. Although there is some uncertainty about the interpretation of certain portions of this section (the differences between interpretation C and interpretation D), it is clear that Christ is the center of the passage. As the center of the Scriptures, the crucified and risen one is also the center of what we believe.

2. This important principle of interpretation recognizes that the Scriptures are the Word of God rather than the word of any human.

3. Because of the forgiveness and righteousness God's people have from Jesus Christ, the church will always stand secure, even in the worst of times and when the worst of its enemies seems to prosper the most. God will deliver His people from all who oppress them.

Closing

Follow the suggestion in the study guide.

Lesson 12

Daniel's Final Vision (Part 1)

The Class Session

Have volunteers read "Theme Verse," "Goal," and "What's Going On Here?"

Searching the Scriptures

Introduction to the Vision

1. Since Daniel was taken into captivity as a youth in 605, and since the

third year of Cyrus is dated 536, the prophet would have been a very old man at the time he experienced this final vision. The vision is dated to call to mind the fact that it was the edict of Cyrus that allowed God's people to return to their homeland. This is significant in that the vision of these concluding chapters deals with how the land and people of Judah would fare under various foreign rulers. Also this chapter and the role of Cyrus in biblical history demonstrate how the Lord controls even unbelieving rulers for the good of His people.

2. Daniel's mourning and fasting may have been caused by news of the difficulties the people of God were having in restoring the Promised Land to its proper state. Since much of the rest of these chapters treats the subject of how the Lord cares for His people as they face opposition from others to their efforts to live according to His will, it is a likely conjecture that the obstacles to the Judeans' rebuilding the temple of God were the cause of Daniel's mourning and fasting. Anointing of the body with oil is a soothing and refreshing practice for people living in the hot and dry climate of the Near East, and refraining from doing so was a sign of great sorrow.

3. In **verse 1** we are assured that what was revealed to Daniel is true, deals with the conflict or suffering of God's people, and was given to him by means of a vision.

The Heavenly Messenger

1. The impressive appearance of the messenger certainly indicated that he had come from heaven. However, because he stated that he had been sent by another and especially because he indicated that the angel Michael had to come to help him, it is unlikely that Daniel had been granted a manifestation of God Himself (as was the case in the vision of **chapter 7**). Instead, an angel other than Michael is the most likely identification of the one who appeared to Daniel on this occasion.

2. The reactions of the companions of Daniel and of Saul indicate that the appearance of the exalted being was not intended for them. As the appearance of the risen Lord was intended only for Saul, so the vision of **Daniel 10–12** was only for the eyes of the prophet.

3. Daniel's reaction in the presence of the angel was one that is paralleled elsewhere in Scripture. This is a natural reaction on the part of a sinful mortal who is suddenly in the presence of one of the God's holy angels.

Preparation for the Vision

1. The angel comforted Daniel by raising him from the ground, calling him a man who was greatly beloved by God, inviting him to stand in his presence, exhorting him not to be afraid, and informing him that his prayers on behalf of the people of God had been answered. All of this

showed the prophet that God was his Savior and so was not displeased with him.

2. The angels of God are assigned by Him to watch over His people ("guardian angels"). The fact that Michael is "your prince" (**10:21;** the Hebrew uses the plural form of *your*) means that he is the patron angel of the people of God. This is a word of encouragement for God's people. Likewise, the "prince of Persia" is the evil "patron angel" of the unbelieving kingdom of Persia. In the Bible the false gods of the unbelieving nations are identified with the demons, that is, with the fallen, evil angels (**Deuteronomy 32:17; Psalm 106:36–37; 1 Corinthians 10:20; Revelation 9:20**).

3. When the Old Testament makes reference to the "latter days," this is a way of indicating that the matter under discussion pertains to the New Testament era (the coming of Christ, the age of the church, the last days, and the like). As we study the vision of these chapters in detail (particularly beginning with **11:36**), we will see that this vision does pertain also to the times of the New Testament age.

4. Daniel fell to the ground unable to speak, and later he confessed the anguish, lack of strength, and even lack of breath he felt. He also indicated that he was unworthy even to speak with the angel. Yet the angel consoled him by restoring to him the ability to speak in his presence. To strengthen Daniel further the angel again touched him and gave him strength. Then the angel bid him not to be afraid and to be strong, calling him one who was esteemed by God and granting him peace, harmony with God.

5. The angel's words implied that he would defeat the "prince" of Persia, after which the prince of Greece would arise on the scene. Michael and the angel speaking here were instrumental in the defeat of Babylon (in the first year of Darius the Mede) and would now also overthrow Persia and Greece. This is a message of encouragement for God's people, for no matter what powerful nations oppress and control them, their guardian angels, given them by God, will always look after their well-being.

The Vision Itself

Have a member of the class read this paragraph before proceeding with the remainder of the study.

Persia and Greece

1. Since Cyrus was currently reigning as king of Persia, the fourth king to succeed him would be Xerxes, known as Ahasuerus in the Bible (as in the book of Esther). He acquired great wealth, which he used to amass an army with which he attempted to conquer Greece.

2. The "mighty king" was Alexander the Great. His empire was eventually

divided into four major parts. He was not succeeded by any of his posterity, and none of his successors ever attained to a might even close to his.

Egypt and Syria

1. After many years the son of Ptolemy I and the grandson of Seleucus I made an alliance in which the daughter of the king of Egypt (Ptolemy II) became the wife of the king of Syria (Antiochus II). After the death of Ptolemy II, the first wife of Antiochus II murdered her former husband and his second wife, so that the alliance accomplished nothing.

2. Ptolemy III of Egypt successfully attacked and took plunder from Syria. Seleucus II of Syria was unsuccessful in his subsequent attempt to attack Egypt.

3. The sons mentioned in **11:10** are Seleucus III and Antiochus III, both sons of Seleucus II. Seleucus III soon died, leaving his brother to wage war with Egypt, hence the change from plural to singular in this verse in Hebrew. Ptolemy IV was at first victorious **(11:11–12)**, but later he was defeated by Antiochus III, when the latter came with an even larger army **(11:13)**.

4. **Daniel 11:14** foretold the rebellion of some Egyptians against Ptolemy IV and the subsequent attempt by some of the Jews to cast off the rule of Ptolemy V. The following verses report how Antiochus III would regain some of the territory he had lost, capturing the city of Sidon (the "fortified city" of **verse 15**) and the land of Palestine ("the Beautiful Land" of **verse 16**), which he took in 198 B.C.

5. **Daniel 11:17** foretold the unsuccessful attempt of Antiochus III to gain some advantage by giving his daughter to be the wife of Ptolemy V. **Verse 18** indicates that Antiochus attempted to conquer part of Asia Minor but was rebuffed by a Roman officer ("commander"). **Daniel 11:19** describes how Antiochus returned home after this incident in defeat.

6. This verse briefly predicts that Seleucus IV of Syria would send a tax collector into Palestine and shortly thereafter would die.

The Word for Us

1. Class members may share what they find reassuring about God using His armies of angels to work on behalf of His people.

2. Incorrect teachings about angels, common in the closing decade of the 20th century, may cause one to think that he or she has the care of God's angels apart from saving faith in Jesus Christ. In seeking the aid of angels apart from Christ, one may actually be falling under the influence of the fallen angels, that is, the devils.

3. Participants may share their insights as to how this aspect of God's

care is comforting to them.

Closing

Follow the suggestion in the study guide.

Lesson 13

Daniel's Final Vision (Part 2)

The Class Session

Have volunteers read "Theme Verses," "Goal," and "What's Going On Here?"

Searching the Scriptures

Antiochus Epiphanes

1. Antiochus was not the legitimate heir to the throne of Syria. He gained dominion over the kingdom by intrigue.

2. For a time Antiochus and Ptolemy acted as friends and attempted something of an alliance. However, their mistrust of one another and evil plotting against each other led to their downfall. The conclusion of this verse indicates that the failure of their evil designs was due ultimately to the fact that it was so determined in advance by God.

3. On his final campaign against Egypt, Antiochus found himself against greater odds than he could overcome, for Egypt had allied itself with the emerging power of Rome. The phrase translated "ships of the western coastlands" (11:30) is literally "ships of Kittim." In the Bible Kittim refers to Cyprus or anyplace to the west. The reference in this instance is to the Romans who foiled the attempt of Antiochus to gain mastery over Egypt. Rebuffed, he returned homeward, venting his wrath against the Jews, among whom he wished to set up a Hellenistic state and the worship of Greek gods. "To those who [forsook] the holy covenant" he gave preferential treatment.

4. By force Antiochus defiled the temple, as he set up the worship of Olympian Zeus (with its orgiastic rituals), and put an end to the daily burnt offering. The Hebrew form of the name of the ancient Canaanite god Baal ("Baal of the Heavens") can be converted by a sort of code into the Hebrew words for "abomination of desolation" which is the literal translation of

the phrase at the end of **11:31**. Thus it seems likely that the phrase "abomination of desolation" refers to a statue of Zeus, in the likeness of Baal, that was set up by Antiochus in the temple.

The immediate reference of Jesus' words is to one or more attempts (successful or otherwise) by the Romans to defile the Jerusalem temple by bringing the worship of God to an end and/or establishing in the temple some form of pagan worship (prior to or in conjunction with the fall of Jerusalem to the Romans in A.D. 70). However, the rest of our Lord's teaching in **Matthew 24** makes it plain that He (and Daniel's words) had referenced the horrible times that the people of God would face throughout history prior to the end of the world.

From Antiochus to Antichrist

1. It is characteristic of Antichrist that he is opposed to the true God and, in fact, to every god. He will have success until the "time of wrath is completed" **(11:36)**, that is, until the end, when he has completed his acts of evil against God. He has his period of prosperity because it "has been determined" by God. (When the Scriptures state that something has been done but do not indicate the agent who has done it, the implication very often is that the thing has been done by God [this is especially true when the passive voice is used]. A similar example is found in **Daniel 11:27**.)

2. We see here that Antichrist rewards with honor and power those who succumb to his enticements and follow him.

The Defeat of Antichrist

1. The appearance of Antichrist is a sign of the end times in which we have been living since the resurrection of Christ and the coming of the Holy Spirit. **Daniel 11:40** indicates this by referring to "the time of the end." It is a time of great warfare as Jesus indicated the end times would be **(Matthew 24:6)**, in which Antichrist is also involved (indicated, for example, in **Revelation 16:12–14**).

2. The "Beautiful Land" is God's people, the church, against whom Antichrist wages his warfare. Edom, Moab, and Ammon were three enemies of God's people from ancient times. Thus, they became symbols of all the enemies of God's people. The fact Moab did not exist as a political entity at the time of Antiochus is a further indication that these verses are not speaking of any historical events but are using symbols to describe what takes place throughout the history of the church on earth.

3. The beautiful holy mountain (Zion) is another symbol for the church, which Antichrist keeps attacking. He will have no one to help him escape his destruction, for he will be put to an end by Christ Himself when He comes in judgment on the Last Day.

The Deliverance of the People of God

Daniel 12:2 is one of the Old Testament's most explicit references to the resurrection of the dead and eternal life. Those who trust in the Lamb who was slain for them will be clothed in His righteousness; they will rise to everlasting life. Those who reject Him will be judged for their sins and experience "shame and everlasting contempt."

The Conclusion of the Prophecy

1. In order to designate the solemnity of his answer the angel took an oath, swearing by the Lord ("Him who lives forever"). The expression "time, times and half a time" of **12:7** corresponds to the three and one-half times of **7:25.** Since three and one-half is only one half of the number seven, which symbolizes completeness, the meaning may be that Antichrist and the powers of this world will prevail over the people of God for only a limited time, until the Lord intervenes on their behalf on the Last Day and the "power of [that is, over] the holy people has been finally broken."

Another possible explanation of this phrase is that Antichrist has power at the beginning (time), after which his power and success doubles (times), but only with the result that his power is vastly diminished (half a time). Whichever of these interpretations is the correct one, the passage still comforts God's people with the thought that God will bring their oppression to an end.

2. The wise, that is, believers, will understand that the people of God will suffer at the hand of those who continue to be wicked. But the wise will also understand that their suffering is but a prelude to their glory in the resurrection.

3. Daniel was instructed to go about his business until the end of time. He would rest in the grave (as will all people), but as one of the wise he will "rise to receive [his] allotted inheritance" in the resurrection from the dead on the Last Day. The comment made on this verse by C. F. Keil, a great German Lutheran interpreter of the 19th century, has often been quoted, "Well shall it be for us if in the end of our days we too are able to depart hence with such consolation of hope" (*Biblical Commentary on the Book of Daniel*, Eerdmans, 1959, p. 506). We shall because of Christ, the firstfruits of those who have fallen asleep, to whom we belong by way of Baptism and through faith, receive eternal life.

The Word for Us

1. Class members may indicate seeing apocalyptic literature as less confusing and intimidating and more reassuring and comforting.

2. Participants may share responses as time and interest permit.

Closing

Follow the suggestion in the study guide.